Bob Garner's

GUIDE TO
NORTH CAROLINA
BARBECUE

Also by Bob Garner

North Carolina Barbecue: Flavored by Time

JOHN F. BLAIR, PUBLISHER   WINSTON-SALEM, NORTH CAROLINA

Bob Garner's

GUIDE TO
NORTH CAROLINA
BARBECUE

by Bob Garner

Published by John F. Blair, Publisher

Copyright© 2002 by Bob Garner
All rights reserved under International
and Pan American Copyright Conventions

Second Printing, 2003

*The paper in this book meets the guidelines
for permanence and durability of the
Committee on Production Guidelines for
Book Longevity of the Council on Library Resources*

Library of Congress Cataloging-in-Publication Data
Garner, Bob, 1946–
Bob Garner's guide to North Carolina barbecue / by Bob Garner.
      p.   cm.
ISBN 0-89587-254-4
1. Barbecue cookery—North Carolina. 2. Restaurants—North
Carolina—Guidebooks. I. Title: Guide to North Carolina barbecue. II. Title.
TX840.B3 G364 2002
641.5'784—dc21
2002010736

Printed in Canada

*Author photograph on the front cover by Martin Tucker
Book design by Debra Long Hampton
Composition by The Roberts Group*

*Dedicated to
the memory of the late pit masters
Ike Green and Lockey Reynolds,
who kept the fires alive
for so many years.*

TABLE OF CONTENTS

Acknowledgments

I want to express my profound gratitude to the many people who contributed to this book in various ways. It would not have been possible without them.

First, I extend my thanks to my friends at UNC-TV for their vital role in the production and broadcast of several programs that made me known to thousands of North Carolinians as "the barbecue man." I'm also grateful to the North Carolina Pork Council and to Neese's Country Sausage for their generous underwriting.

I would like to express appreciation to Greta Lint and the Lexington Tourism Authority and to photographer Dan Routh for allowing me to use several photographs. Special thanks are also due to Ed Mitchell of Wilson and "Russ" Russell of Windsor for their assistance in this department.

To my friend Keith Allen of Chapel Hill, thanks for helping me meet my "pig picking" responsibilities while I was working on the book and for upholding the standard of North Carolina barbecue for so many years. Gratitude is also due my brother-in-law Tad Everett for his interest and assistance.

I want to express special appreciation to those in leadership at

Christ Church in Burlington for taking up the slack while I was so busy with this project.

To my children Anna Barrett, Van, Nelson, Jessica, and Everett, I express my gratitude for their unwavering encouragement, and to my first grandchild, Sadler, I say thanks for bringing us all such joy. Thanks to my Mom, Dorothy, for her quiet belief in me. And finally, I thank my wife Ruthie for her patience, good cheer, help, love, and support in more ways than I can recount.

THREE CENTURIES OF NORTH CAROLINA BARBECUE

In 1924, one of North Carolina's first sit-down barbecue restaurants was opened in Rocky Mount by Bob Melton, who added a room on to the pit shed he had built on the banks of the Tar River two years earlier. At about the same time, Sid Weaver and Jess Swicegood built modest structures to house their competing barbecue places in Lexington. The two had been selling barbecue from side-by-side tents on the courthouse square since 1919.

That period marked the beginning of one of the favorite pastimes in North Carolina: searching for good barbecue joints. (*Restaurant* somehow seems too grand a word for places that began with a few tables and chairs added to the barbecue pits, so customers could sit down to eat the smoked meat they'd ordered, rather than taking it home.) Related—but quite separate— pastimes include cooking barbecue for fun or profit, competitive barbecue cooking, and, most popular of all, discussing barbecue.

THE BEGINNINGS OF A LEGACY

Tar Heels love to talk about barbecue even more than they love to eat it because it's been part of their history and heritage for more than 300 years. The practice of slowly roasting meats over wood coals on a framework of green sticks was documented among the native inhabitants of the West Indies by the mid-1600s. (*Barbacoa* is the Spanish version of a Taino Indian word.) Whether early settlers brought the practice to Virginia or whether this continent's Native Americans already had a similar practice and passed it on to the colonists, we know that by the late 1600s, Virginia had enacted a law banning the discharging of firearms at barbecues. (This was so the colonists would know without confusion that gunfire signaled an imminent Indian attack.)

From the very beginning, barbecue in North Carolina meant pork. During the 1500s, the Spanish introduced pigs to the southeastern part of America. Whereas cattle tended to fare poorly in the region, swine flourished, nowhere more so than in North Carolina. Settlers from Virginia and elsewhere brought more pigs with them to the state. By 1728, William Byrd of Virginia wrote the following about eastern North Carolina: "The only business here is the raising of hogs, which is managed with the least trouble and affords the diet they are most fond of." Byrd went on to note that "the inhabitants of North Carolina devour so much swine's flesh that it fills them full of gross humours."

Newcomers encountering the vinegar-based barbecue sauce common to eastern North Carolina are usually surprised to learn that it is, in fact, America's original barbecue sauce, developed in the region during the late 17th and early 18th centuries. Pork cooked over an open fire was the meat most commonly served, and colonists routinely seasoned it with an ordinary table condiment of the time, which consisted of vinegar, salt, red and black pepper, and oyster juice. (It's my theory that because pigs of that period frequently ate wild acorns or were fed garbage, the pork probably had a fairly strong taste or odor, and that the fiery vinegar mixture may have been intended to make the meat more palatable.) Salty vinegar liberally laced with pepper (but minus the oyster juice!) is still basically the same sauce used on eastern North Carolina barbecue today, even though the quality of our pork is now unparalleled in terms of cleanliness, taste, and leanness.

Years passed between the development of eastern North Carolina barbecue sauce and the type common in the Piedmont region. When the eastern vinegar sauce was developed in the late 1600s, it would never have occurred to anyone to add any sort of tomato extract, since tomatoes were thought at the time to be poisonous. "Love apples," as they were sometimes called, were also thought to be an aphrodisiac, albeit one with an ultimately fatal result. By around 1820, however, tomatoes had been proven safe to eat. By the time the distinctive Lexington-style barbecue and its accompanying "dip" began to become well known in the North Carolina Piedmont, it was a natural thing for tomato ketchup to be added to the traditional vinegar base. (The art of cooking barbecue followed the country's westward expansion. More and more ketchup was added, and barbecue sauces became increasingly thick. Today, the nation's most commonly recognized barbecue sauce is one that's ketchup-based.)

NORTH CAROLINA'S EARLY BARBECUE RESTAURANTS

Cooking real barbecue is something that cannot be rushed. Few of us have the time, energy, patience, or skill to do it ourselves.

Commercial establishments came into being because barbecue has always been one of those foods prepared by a few for the consumption of their neighbors. In North Carolina, barbecuing pigs was generally hands-on work for small farmers, merchants, and their hired helpers, rather than being relegated to slaves, as it was in the more aristocratic states of Virginia and South Carolina. But it was still work that was hot and demanding enough to be undertaken by only a relative handful of people in any given area.

Barbecue was usually purchased as carryout from one or more well-known local cooks, most of whom prepared the meat on weekends over backyard pits. As early as 1830, in the town of Ayden in Pitt County, Skilton Dennis began selling pork barbecue out of the back of a covered wagon. The town was then known as A Den, as in A Den of Thieves. While Dennis no doubt sold plenty of barbecue to the community's unsavory elements, his barbecue wagon was also a regular feature at the area's church camp meetings. Today, two of his descendants, Bum Dennis and Pete Jones, still own and operate barbecue places in Ayden.

There were a few noteworthy early restaurants. Like Bob Melton in Rocky Mount and Sid Weaver and Jess Swicegood in Lexington, Adam Scott of Goldsboro started out selling the meat from whole pigs he cooked on a backyard pit on weekends. Soon, he was serving sit-down meals on the back porch of his house, and by 1933, he had enclosed the porch and turned it into a simple dining room. The unusual thing about Scott—whose restaurant would be enlarged three times before being moved to another location—was that he was black and many of his patrons were white, at a time when blacks and whites practically never sat down together to eat. Scott's black neighbors, farmers from the countryside, and prominent white businessmen and politicians, including Governor J. Melville Broughton, rubbed elbows as they stood in line in Scott's backyard, waiting for a table. (Sadly, his restaurant closed in 2001 because none of his descendants was in a position to carry on the enterprise. The Scott family, however, continues distributing Scott's Famous Barbecue Sauce, sold in grocery stores throughout North Carolina. Adam Scott steadfastly maintained throughout his life that the ingredients for the sauce came to him in a dream.)

Barbecue stands began springing up wherever large numbers of people gathered. Towns with tobacco warehouses, where North Carolina's flue-cured leaf was brought in from the countryside for auction, usually had several barbecue stands. To this day, places such as Rocky Mount, Goldsboro, Wilson, and Greenville are known not only for their once-mighty tobacco markets but also for their barbecue restaurants. Tobacco farmers who had sold their crop and had some cash in their pockets often celebrated the occasion with meals at local barbecue restaurants, a custom that persists today even as North Carolina's tobacco economy declines.

Around the Piedmont town of Lexington during the early 1900s, a few men known for their skill in using hardwood coals to roast pork shoulders (instead of the whole pigs cooked in the east) started out preparing barbecue for special occasions, then began holding occasional public cookouts, which were locally known as "Everybody's Day." Soon, barbecue was also being cooked and sold during the periodic week-long court sessions, during which crowds of people streamed into Lexington from the surrounding countryside. In 1919, the aforementioned Sid Weaver and a partner, George Ridenhour, erected a tent on the courthouse square that became Lexington's first semipermanent barbecue stand. Not long afterward, Lexington barbecue pioneer Jess Swicegood put up a tent adjacent to and in direct competition with Weaver's. Soon, Weaver (having bought out Ridenhour) and Swicegood both moved their businesses to small buildings.

There is some disagreement as to whether Piedmont-style barbecue first gained a foothold in Salsibury, in Rowan County, or in Lexington, in Davidson County. John Blackwelder of Salisbury is said to have added a barbecue pit to his taxi stand in 1918, one year before Sid Weaver erected his barbecue tent on Lexington's courthouse square. Regardless of who was first, the reputation of Lexington's barbecue quickly eclipsed that of Salisbury's.

In 1927, one of North Carolina's most enduring barbecue legacies got under way when high-school student C. Warner Stamey began learning the art of Lexington barbecue while working for Jess Swicegood. By 1930, Stamey had returned to his hometown of Shelby and, following Swicegood's example, opened a barbecue stand in a tent with a sawdust floor. During the next several years, Stamey taught the barbecue business to both his wife's brother, Alston Bridges, and another Shelby resident, Red Bridges (no relation). When Stamey moved back to Lexington in the mid-1930s, Alston Bridges and Red Bridges opened their own barbecue restaurants, establishments that are still going strong today and are known to barbecue enthusiasts nationwide.

In 1938, Stamey bought the Lexington restaurant where he had learned his trade from Jess Swicegood. At that same restaurant in the early 1950s, he taught his barbecue secrets to another young man, Wayne Monk, now the owner of Lexington Barbecue and arguably the best-known barbecue expert in North Carolina. Stamey then moved to Greensboro and opened a restaurant on High Point Road that still occupies the same landmark location (although a newer building) across the street from the Greensboro Coliseum. At about the same time, Stamey began experimenting with serving hush puppies with barbecue, borrowing a food item previously served mainly in fish camps. Until that time, barbecue was routinely served with either slices of white bread or rolls. Today, hush puppies are considered a standard accompaniment to barbecue, unless it's being served on a sandwich.

Chip Stamey, Warner's grandson, now runs the restaurant on High Point Road. Just inside the door is a collection of old photographs documenting the work of Warner Stamey, the man who did more than any other to spread the fame of Lexington-style barbecue.

Barbecue places, like other restaurants, were relatively few and far between in North Carolina until after World War II. Once cars, tires, and gasoline were again available after the rationing of the war years, returning servicemen and their families enjoyed riding up and down newly paved roads searching for the best barbecue. Barbecue sandwiches, hot dogs, and hamburgers were among the most popular foods served at the newly emerging drive-in restaurants. Many of the new drive-ins had barbecue pits. Curb service made it quick and convenient to compare one place's barbecue with another's. Interestingly enough, with the exception of one well-known drive-in chain, just about the only curb service still available in North Carolina is offered by a handful of barbecue places, including the famed Lexington Barbecue. New visitors to "The Monk," as Wayne Monk's place is known locally, are routinely bewildered by the steady chorus of automobile horns, which they invariably mistake for customers disputing possession of parking spaces. Actually, they're announcements of patrons' intentions to place takeout orders.

BARBECUE STYLES 101

This book is a guide to North Carolina barbecue found in restaurants. There is a totally different subculture surrounding pig pickings, which are traditional, whole-hog barbecues at which guests are invited to stand around and pluck succulent morsels of meat from beautifully browned roast pigs. Pig-cooking contests or barbecue cook-offs—which I call "beautiful pig contests"— constitute yet another field of endeavor, one with a large number of faithful enthusiasts, a strict list of rules developed by the North Carolina Pork Council, and a bevy of cash prizes and trophies. Then there's the catered barbecue, which is likely to be a political gathering, and the fund-raising barbecue cooked up by a church, a volunteer fire department, or a police auxiliary, at which barbecue is sold either by the plate or by the pound. Certain characteristics common to all these activities tend to separate North Carolina from other barbecue hot spots around the country—and, indeed, to separate the barbecue found in one region of North Carolina from that found in another. If you're going to get the most out of cruising barbecue joints—or enjoying North Carolina barbecue in any fashion—you need to get acquainted with the basics.

First, you need to become familiar with what's served in North Carolina and how it compares with the barbecue elsewhere. There are really only seven distinct barbecue regions in the United States. Eastern North Carolina and Piedmont North Carolina are two of the seven. The remaining five are South Carolina; western Kentucky; Memphis, Tennessee; Kansas City, Missouri; and Texas. There's a great deal of barbecue available in the rest of the country, to be sure, but you can bet that no matter where you are, the barbecue will imitate one of these regional styles.

It bears repeating that in both the eastern and Piedmont regions of North Carolina, barbecue means pork, though chicken is thrown in as an added attraction from time to time. (It's okay to refer to it as "barbecued chicken," but never simply as "barbecue.") Sure, there are some restaurant chains from out of state that serve Texas-style beef brisket or Memphis-style pulled pork and ribs slathered with thick, sweet tomato sauce, and they may call it all "barbecue." But in the Tar Heel State, east or west, barbecue means pork—usually chopped but sometimes sliced, served with a thin sauce that always begins with a vinegar base and that varies in heat from mild to fiery and in taste from salty to sweet.

In my opinion, North Carolina barbecue is the only type in

which the meat itself is at center stage, rather than the sauce, the degree of heat, or the smoke. Lightly kissed by smoke, rather than overcome by it, North Carolina barbecued pork has a rich, sweet taste. At its best, it is meltingly tender, with attractive flecks of outside brown meat adding a chewier texture.

Quite a few North Carolina barbecue places prepare delicious pork ribs on certain days of the week, and a few may even offer tasty beef brisket as a change of pace, but these dishes are sideshows, the exceptions that prove the unspoken rule that reserves the term *barbecue* for our own beloved pork.

In other states, soft drinks and beer are the beverages of choice to accompany barbecue meals. But in North Carolina, east or Piedmont, the overwhelming favorite is sweet tea over crushed ice, which melts fast enough to cut the sweetness just a bit, providing the perfect balm to the palate after a bite of spicy barbecue. To the best of my knowledge, only one place—Pete Jones's Skylight Inn in Ayden—serves no iced tea, offering customers a couple of choices of bottled soft drinks instead.

There are strong similarities between the barbecue styles of the coastal plain and the Piedmont, especially in comparison to the barbecue found elsewhere in the country. (The mountain region has little in the way of a distinctive barbecue tradition of its own.) However, anyone who wants to be considered knowledgeable on the subject of barbecue (and who wants to explore the barbecue-restaurant landscape) must learn about the great schism between the proponents of the vinegary, whole-hog barbecue of the east and those of the milder, sweeter pork-shoulder barbecue of the Piedmont. In truth, this is a benign family squabble kept alive by the enjoyment derived by both sides. (Then again, it costs us credibility when it comes to claiming that North Carolina barbecue is better than what other states have to offer, since it leaves us vulnerable to the assertion that we can't even agree among ourselves about what constitutes good barbecue.) Most of us are content to assume that North Carolina is barbecue heaven and to continue milking the east-west debate for maximum conversational enjoyment. Since the barbecue preference of most North Carolinians is heavily influenced by where they were raised, and given the increasing mobility of recent decades, there are plenty of eastern-barbecue enthusiasts scattered throughout the Piedmont and vice versa, so continuing discord appears to be safe for the foreseeable future.

EASTERN NORTH CAROLINA BARBECUE

East of U.S. 1, barbecue means not only pork but the whole hog. What difference could this possibly make to the casual restaurant patron? Well, pork has both dark and white meat, much like chicken, and cooking the whole hog means that the chopped barbecue will include both the dark meat from the shoulders and the rib area and the nearly white meat from the hams, loins, and tenderloins. The dark meat is more moist because of its higher fat content, while the white meat is leaner and therefore drier. Overall, eastern North Carolina barbecue tends to be drier than that found in the Piedmont because of the inclusion of so much white meat in the chopped mixture.

Then, too, many of the high-volume eastern barbecue houses have begun chopping their barbecue by machine, giving the meat a finer texture and also drying it out somewhat. James Vilas, writing for *Esquire* some years ago, described the eastern product as "dry, salty barbecue."

Incidentally, historians believe the custom of chopping barbecue originated because so many people, especially older adults, used to have bad teeth and couldn't chew the meat otherwise. Thoughtful hosts who wanted to make sure that even their oldest guests were properly looked after started serving the meat, in effect, pre-chewed. Rocky Mount has a reputation for serving the most finely minced barbecue. In the 1950s, a friendly debate was carried on in the Rocky Mount and Goldsboro newspapers over which of the towns had the better barbecue. Henry Belk, then editor of the *Goldsboro News-Argus*, wrote that Rocky Mount's barbecue "has some resemblance to mush." Bob Melton's, in business in Rocky Mount since 1924, serves barbecue chopped to a consistency I won't call mushy, but which, let us say, could be thoroughly enjoyed by an absolutely toothless person.

Barbecue in the coastal plain is seasoned with its historic sauce of vinegar, water, salt, black pepper, and both finely ground and crushed red pepper. There are thousands of variations on this basic mixture, and a particular sauce may have a dozen other "secret" spices, but the main taste sensation is of hot, salty vinegar. A true eastern sauce not only contains no tomato ketchup or paste but also has no added sugar, molasses, corn syrup, or other sweeteners. Some coastal-plain cooks do add sugar to smooth out a "table" sauce or a dipping sauce for the chunks of meat pulled off at a pig picking. But they usually omit the sweetener from the sauce used both for basting the pig as it cooks and for seasoning chopped barbecue.

Barbecue and fried chicken are often served together in combination plates or family-style dinners throughout eastern North Carolina. Sometimes, barbecued chicken is offered in combination with the chopped pork. There's no real consistency to this dish, which ranges from poultry that's pit-cooked over live coals and basted with vinegar-based sauce to chicken that's first covered with thick, red sauce, then baked in an oven.

Brunswick stew is another common accompaniment to barbecue in the eastern third of North Carolina. Believed to have been developed in Virginia but also claimed by the residents of Brunswick, Georgia, this dish originally contained squirrel meat and stale bread but is now most often made with chicken, pork, tomatoes, cream-style corn, lima beans, and onions. Some cooks stay within acceptable bounds by adding diced potatoes, while others stray into questionable territory by adding snap beans, garden peas, beef, and who knows what else. The perfect Brunswick stew, in my opinion, is thick, creamy, and sweet enough to perfectly balance the piquancy of the eastern-style barbecue with which it's consumed.

Coleslaw and boiled potatoes are also likely to find their way on to an eastern North Carolina barbecue plate. The slaw will be either white or yellow in color, moistened with vinegar and/or mayonnaise and/or mustard and sweetened by the addition of sugar and/or chopped sweet pickles. The potatoes may be stewed with onions until they're slightly thickened, or they may have some ketchup, hot sauce, or paprika added to the liquid. Both side dishes, like Brunswick stew, are meant to be either sweet enough or bland enough in taste to complement the spicy heat and saltiness of the barbecue.

Barbecue sandwiches, served on soft, white buns and topped with coleslaw, are not quite as prevalent in the east as they are in the Piedmont, primarily because easterners are, as a group, extraordinarily fond of corn bread. With a coastal-plain barbecue plate, you'll get either deep-fried hush puppies or corn sticks, which are 10-inch sticks of corn bread baked in a trapezoid-shaped mold until they're partially cooked, then delivered frozen to restaurants, where they're deep-fried. (I highly recommend the practice of using a corn stick as an edible spoon to consume your favorite Brunswick stew!) A few places serve squares of flat, baked corn bread laced with pork drippings as a barbecue accompaniment.

Lexington-Style Barbecue

Lexington-style barbecue, occasionally referred to as Piedmont or western barbecue, is prepared by slow-roasting only the pork shoulder (the hog's front legs), rather than the whole pig. The shoulder is part of the dark portion of the pig's meat, compared to the white meat of the hams and loins, and is more suffused with pockets of fat, so Lexington barbecue tends to be more moist than its eastern counterpart, even after all visible fat has been removed.

Lexington barbecue is nearly always hand-chopped by cleaver, rather than by machine, and tends to have a coarser or chunkier texture than eastern barbecue. Nearly all Piedmont barbecue houses also offer coarse-chopped meat, which is basically cut into cubes, and sliced barbecue. Neither of these is ordinarily available in the east.

Lexington-style barbecue is also distinguished in that an especially prized portion of the meat known as "outside brown" can usually be requested. A pork shoulder trimmed and ready for barbecuing is partially covered by skin and fat, but a significant portion of the surface is exposed red meat. Once a shoulder has been pit-cooked over wood coals for between 10 and 16 hours, this exposed surface meat turns a deep reddish brown hue, becomes chewy in texture, and is heavily infused with the flavor of wood smoke. At most Lexington-style barbecue places, you can request that your order be made up partially or entirely of outside brown.

A fair number of barbecue places in the Piedmont offer Brunswick stew, although it is not nearly as common an accompaniment to barbecue as it is in the east and tends to disappear as you travel farther west. Boiled potatoes are virtually unheard of as a barbecue side dish in the Piedmont. They're replaced on quite a few menus by baked beans.

Throughout the Piedmont, barbecue sauce is known as "dip." It is generally sweeter than the eastern version, due to the addition of brown or white sugar, and usually contains ketchup. But even given the addition of a small amount of tomato, Lexington dip is still much thinner and more tart-tasting than the thick, red barbecue sauces found on grocery-store shelves and is technically still a vinegar-based, rather than a tomato-based, sauce, contrary to the assertions of most easterners. If eastern sauce tends to taste like hot, salty vinegar, Lexington dip might be described as a thin sweet-and-sour sauce. And whereas eastern chopped barbecue tends to arrive at the table already liberally seasoned with vinegar, salt, and red pepper, the Lexington version may or may not have been moistened with sauce when it's served. In the Piedmont, nearly every barbecue-house table holds a bottle of Texas Pete Hot Sauce, so customers can adjust the heat to their own liking. Many barbecue places offer both hot and mild versions of their sauces.

Catawba College history professor Gary Freeze has a well-developed, if unproven, theory that the barbecue practices of the Piedmont were heavily influenced by the German immigrants who came south from Pennsylvania to North Carolina by way of Virginia's Shenandoah Valley. Freeze's research into the hog-butchering practices of the Pennsylvania Germans (which were different from the English methods practiced in the coastal plain) suggests that the pork shoulder was one of their favorite cuts of meat, and that it was usually braised in a fruit-flavored liquid not dissimilar in taste to Lexington barbecue sauce. Freeze points out that many of the best-known early barbecue experts in the Piedmont had German names—Weaver, Ridenhour, and Swicegood, for example—and that some of the earliest Piedmont barbecuing was done in heavily German cotton-mill villages.

One of Jess Swicegood's descendants tells a different version of the origin of Lexington-style dip. According to this fanciful-sounding tale, Swicegood was once enjoying a dinner of barbecued rabbit doused with ketchup, accompanied by a serving of greens saturated with vinegar. The story goes that the ketchup and vinegar ran together on the plate, giving Swicegood the idea for a sauce that might taste good on barbecued pork shoulder.

Much of the debate between east and west revolves around Lexington-style barbecue coleslaw, which is reddish in color and moistened with the same ingredients that go into barbecue sauce: vinegar, ketchup, sugar, and pepper. Barbecue slaw is often tangier than the meat itself, so whereas an eastern sandwich may have a mild slaw added to balance the fieriness of the chopped meat, a Piedmont sandwich usually spices up the relatively mild meat with coleslaw possessing a peppery bite. Many Piedmont barbecue restaurants offer white coleslaw in addition to barbecue slaw.

Hush puppies vary in size, texture, and sweetness from place to place throughout the Piedmont, but by and large, they're very similar to those found in eastern barbecue establishments. Quite a number of Piedmont barbecue joints offer dinner rolls as an alternative to hush puppies.

The barbecue tray, absent from the east, is a fixture in the Piedmont. A tray is simply a small rectangular container, usually made from gray recycled paper, which contains chopped barbecue on one side and coleslaw on the other. Basically, you order a barbecue plate if you want meat, slaw, and French fries, whereas the less expensive tray doesn't come with fries. Both include hush puppies or rolls.

BARBECUE'S FIVE OTHER REGIONAL TYPES

Though barbecue developed in the Southeast, along the Mississippi River, and in Texas, the popularity of meat that's smoked and/or served with a sweet and spicy sauce has spread to all parts of the country. But the barbecue found in every other area of the country closely reflects the cooking methods and sauces that evolved in only five areas, aside from eastern and Piedmont North Carolina. You'll take greater enjoyment in sampling the country's various types of barbecue if you learn the basic characteristics of each and learn to speak the local barbecue dialect of wherever you happen to be.

SOUTH CAROLINA

In South Carolina, barbecue is prepared from both the whole hog and the shoulder. Around the edges of the state, much of it is served with a thicker version of the sauce popular in the North Carolina Piedmont. However, in the central region of the state, wood-cooked barbecue is traditionally served with a startling regional peculiarity: mustard-based sauce. Containing either sugar, syrup, or molasses to cut the tartness of the mustard, and ranging in color from bright to dull yellow, this sauce also contains vinegar, salt, spices, plenty of red pepper, and sometimes ketchup.

Another notable South Carolina specialty—found nowhere else, to my knowledge—is barbecue hash, which is traditionally served over rice as an accompaniment to pork barbecue. Also known as pork hash or liver hash, this dish is essentially a thick gravy with onions, devised to use up the pig's organ meats. Nowadays, hog jowls are used instead of organ meats in most of the Palmetto State's barbecue hash.

WESTERN KENTUCKY

In the western end of Kentucky, just across the Ohio River from Indiana, mutton, the meat of mature sheep, is favored for barbecue. Sheep grazing has been prevalent in the area since the early 19th century, and holding mutton barbecues has been a favorite activity of several Catholic parishes in the vicinity of Owensboro since the 1830s, first as social events and later as fund-raisers. Sauces include a mild tomato-based version; "black dip," which is heavily flavored with Worcestershire; and a peppery-hot topping. Sandwiches are typically topped with an onion slice and a pickle, rather than coleslaw. The favorite side dish is Burgoo, a spicy stew containing chopped mutton. Burgoo bears some resemblance to Brunswick stew.

The city of Owensboro, which fancies itself "the Barbecue Capital of the World," holds a large barbecue festival each year, known to some as "the Burning of Owensboro." It features a large cinder-block barbecue pit erected down the center of a main city street.

MEMPHIS, TENNESSEE

Memphis is the home of the world's largest barbecue festival and competition, Memphis in May. The city has nearly 100 barbecue restaurants, which primarily serve "pulled" meat (in hunks) from pork shoulders, as well as pork ribs. Heavy smoking is characteristic of Memphis-style barbecue. The meat is frequently cooked in a chamber adjacent to the wood fire, through which smoke circulates, rather than directly over hardwood coals, as is the case with North Carolina barbecue. Ribs are typically served either "wet," meaning heavily sauced, or "dry," meaning that they've been treated before cooking with a dry spice rub but have had no sauce applied. Dry ribs are sometimes dipped into a side container of sauce and sometimes enjoyed with no sauce at all.

The favored sauce for both ribs and pulled pork is a thick, red, tangy version, although a variety of different table sauces are offered in some restaurants.

Kansas City, Missouri

In Kansas City, beef, pork, chicken, and other meats are more or less equally valued for barbecuing. "If it moves, we cook it" is the motto of the Kansas City Barbecue Society, which sanctions hundreds of barbecue cookoffs all across America. The American Royal, held every October, is considered the World Series of barbecue contests, with some 380 teams entering both invitational and open divisions. Approximately 75 barbecue restaurants—including such legendary spots as Arthur Bryant's (famous for the "burnt ends" of its beef briskets), Gates Barbecue, and Smokestack Barbecue—offer beef brisket, ribs, pork shoulder, chicken, and sausage, anointed with sauces ranging from pepper-vinegar to supersweet molasses-and-tomato mixtures.

Texas

Throughout Texas, beef brisket (a rectangular cut approximately three inches thick) is the number-one choice for barbecue, although Texans are also fond of barbecued pork ribs, pork shoulder, chicken, and even sausage.

Briskets weighing approximately 10 pounds apiece are smoked for hours in indirect-heat chambers. Wood ranging from mesquite to oak serves as fuel. A perfectly done beef brisket is dark, dark brown on the outside and has a reddish layer known as a "smoke ring" encircling the meat just below the surface. The beef is sliced diagonally across the grain and served with a variety of thick sauces. It is usually accompanied by baked beans, creamy white coleslaw, and either grilled "Texas toast" or slices of plain white loaf bread.

The practice of slow-smoking Texas beef barbecue wasn't perfected by cowboys on the open range, as you might imagine, but rather by butchers of German ancestry who settled in the Texas hill country and cooked and sold barbecue as a way to entice customers to buy tough, relatively undesirable cuts of beef.

WOOD COOKING VERSUS GAS OR ELECTRICITY

North Carolina Department of Agriculture regulations stipulate that pork cooked over gas flames or in an electric cooker cannot be labeled "barbecue" if it's packaged for sale in stores; instead, it has to be labeled "cooked pork." No such regulations, however, apply to barbecue restaurants. As a result, much of what's served as "barbecue" in eateries across the state is no longer cooked over real wood coals.

The expense of wood, the mess caused by smoke and soot, and the hard work of building fires and shoveling coals are all reasons why so many restaurateurs have stopped cooking with wood. Another reason is that local health departments can make it very tough or even impossible for the owners of barbecue places who try to maintain the old ways. Several restaurant owners have told me that cooking with wood, even if it's allowed, automatically results in a three- or four-point reduction on North Carolina's 100-point sanitation rating scale, and that if even one or two other minor problems are found, the restaurant will be facing the loss of its grade-A rating. (Personally, I think many health-department inspectors won't be satisfied until everything we eat is plucked straight from the freezer, then immediately cooked into submission in a microwave oven.)

Another important factor is that, at least in eastern North Carolina, consumers of barbecue no longer expect a wood-smoked taste. Many people who cook their own whole-hog barbecue have switched to propane-fueled cookers because of their relative ease and convenience, and they'll tell you with a straight face, "Most folks really can't tell the difference." Most of the winners of the state's various pig-cooking contests now cook with gas, having realized that the judges are no longer giving credit for a smoked favor. To many, the sauce and the seasonings, rather than the wood smoke, are the elements that give barbecue its taste and character. So many restaurant customers have blithely accepted a change from wood to gas or electricity—all the time claiming, "The barbecue is as good as it's always been"—that you can hardly blame the owners for not being willing to undertake the extra work.

Genuine pit cooking using wood is much more common in the Piedmont, perhaps because barbecue in this industrialized region is more widely regarded as a way of paying homage to a simpler past and staying in touch with the state's heritage. People visiting well-known barbecue restaurants in the Piedmont are used to seeing clouds of bluish white smoke billowing from the pits and enjoying the entrancing aroma that comes only from the fat of roasting pork dripping onto hardwood coals. The lack of a visible woodpile or brick chimney is, with a few notable exceptions, considered a competitive disadvantage.

Let me hasten to say that of the four characteristics of great barbecue—tenderness, seasoning, consistency, and smoked flavor—only the delicate taste obtained by cooking over hardwood coals cannot be obtained through use of a gas or electric cooker. I have eaten a lot of good barbecue that wasn't wood-cooked, and I have eaten some very mediocre barbecue that *was* cooked in a pit. While I personally prefer the bewitching aroma and taste of hardwood smoke, I appreciate the tenderness, texture, and complex seasoning of some of the best electric- or gas-cooked barbecue I've been privileged to enjoy. While there are curmudgeons who grumpily insist, "If it isn't cooked on wood, it isn't barbecue," I say life is too short for such ideological rigidity.

In the pages that follow, I present my personal choices of the 100 best places to eat barbecue in North Carolina. Obviously, almost every single reader would have made a few different choices. And on anybody's list of 100 of anything, there are probably 10 to 15 entries that could arguably have been replaced by an equal number that weren't included. I don't consider myself a restaurant critic, since I recognize my opinion isn't better than anyone else's. So rather than say something uncomplimentary about a place, I'd rather say nothing at all and leave it at that. Let me urge you, however, not to conclude that a place is substandard because it isn't included here. I could very easily have made an honest mistake (and probably did). I do believe all the places that *are* included have something significant to recommend them. My most sincere wishes are that you'll have fun using my guide and that it will help you come up with your own list of North Carolina's top 100 barbecue places.

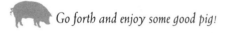 *Go forth and enjoy some good pig!*

Bob Garner's

GUIDE TO
NORTH CAROLINA
BARBECUE

Snooks Old Fashion Barbecue occupies a small complex on a busy corner of U.S. 158 west of Winston-Salem.

SNOOKS OLD FASHION BARBECUE
109 Junie Beauchamp Road
Advance, N.C. 27006
336-998-4305
Lunch and dinner Tuesday through Saturday

Snooks Old Fashion Barbecue is located in an unusual gaggle of buildings on U.S. 158, just southwest of Hillsdale, Clemmons, and Winston-Salem. Located on a busy corner, this complex includes one building that is apparently an unused country store. Nearby is a kitchen and enclosed takeout window. In the third building, you'll find a dining room and in the fourth are rest rooms. The rest of the complex includes a barbecue pit, complete with woodpile, and various storage buildings and sheds. It seems the present kitchen/takeout building used to be the original barbecue pit, which was built over fifty years ago. Rather than getting into major

3

renovations when he built a new pit, the present owner simply added small, freestanding buildings and sheds as needed.

Once you receive your order from the takeout window, you can either go into a separate building, which contains counters and stools and dining tables, or you can eat *al fresco* at one of the picnic tables.

The food at this picturesque establishment enjoys a strong reputation among the local residents, although one lady mused earnestly that she thought the barbecue prepared twice a year by the nearby Advance Fire Department was "just a little better."

Well, let's face it: no commercial establishment is ever going to win a barbecue face-off with *any* local fire department. But suffice it to say that Snooks Old Fashion Barbecue serves an excellent, wood-cooked barbecue, with a mild, savory flavor as opposed to either a sweet or tangy vinegar taste. Dozens of day-glo signs tacked up outside the takeout window advertise every conceivable type of sandwich. The burgers are the biggest sellers, next to barbecue, and the management is proud of the fact that the burgers are made only with freshly ground local meat. No frozen processed stuff from who knows where comes onto the premises. There are lots of other goodies, too. A wide, appetizing selection of fresh vegetables is available in season, and all the desserts are homemade, including strawberry cream-cheese pie, chocolate cream-cheese pound cake, and chocolate meringue pie.

Snooks is located across the road from an interesting-looking store that features antiques and collectibles, which may indicate that you can have a quality dining *and* shopping experience. Even if you're not interested in shopping, Snooks, which is located just off Interstate 40, is well worth a slight detour. To get there, take Exit 180 off Interstate 40 at Hillsdale and turn west on to U.S. 158. The restaurant is 2.3 miles on the left.

Albemarle's Log Cabin Bar-B-Que is a real pit-cooker.

LOG CABIN BAR-B-QUE
2322 U.S. 52 North
Albemarle, N.C. 28001
704-982-5257
Lunch and dinner Monday through Saturday

As you might expect from its name, Log Cabin Bar-B-Que is located in a rustic, brown-painted log building on the northern outskirts of Albemarle. When I first visited several years ago, I found the pit master working at outdoor, wood-burning pits. The pits have been enclosed since then, taking away some of the atmosphere but none of the taste of pork shoulders and chicken pit-cooked over real hickory wood.

Inside this roomy, cheerful restaurant is a long, attractive wood counter, stained dark, with a blue Formica top. This color scheme is repeated in the booths lining the walls. As you might expect in this region of the state, there are quite a few NASCAR posters on the walls, but the large picture of golden-brown pork shoulders roasting on a pit showcases the real attraction at Log Cabin.

Because of some family connections, there are some similarities between this restaurant and Whispering Pines Bar-B-Que, which is just down the street toward town.

Both serve intensely flavored, wood-cooked barbecue and an unusually peppery sauce that resembles a lively eastern sauce more than the Lexington-style dip that's more prevalent in the Piedmont. The iced tea at both restaurants is mixed so that it isn't overly sweet. At Log Cabin, a full pitcher of the flavorful nectar is found on every occupied table.

Despite other similarities, Log Cabin has a recipe for hush puppies that's different from that found at Whispering Pines. Here they're golf-ball size and have a smooth, golden-brown exterior, as compared to the grainy, crusty pups at Whispering Pines. I enjoyed creamy, white coleslaw, something of a contrast to the tart barbecue slaw at the other restaurant.

Log Cabin offers specials every day. On the Wednesday I visited, I tried the pit-cooked barbecued chicken, which came to the table with a wonderful, smoky aroma wafting up from the plate. It was as tender and delicious as it appeared.

There's a good selection of homemade desserts. During my visit, the selection included chocolate pound cake, lemon Sundrop cake, and chocolate brownies.

This is, quite simply, one of the best barbecue restaurants in this part of the state, and it's worth driving quite a bit out of the way to give it a try.

WHISPERING PINES BAR-B-QUE

1421 U.S. 52 North
Albemarle, N.C. 28001
704-982-6184
Lunch and dinner Tuesday through Saturday

Located in a tiny building with a steep pitched roof, Whispering Pines Bar-B-Que looks a little like a mountain chalet perched beside U.S. 52 North in Albemarle. The tall, triangular sign, emblazoned with a pine tree, tells passersby it's been here since 1945. Inside the compact, pine-paneled dining room, there are eight or ten stools at the counter and maybe a half-dozen booths painted bright green and yellow.

While the physical dimensions aren't large inside Whispering Pines, the place is known for some of the biggest servings of barbecue in the entire state. Lonnie Doby started out cooking on real, wood-burning pits at the end of World War II. While the

Whispering Pines Bar-B-Que barbecues with wood on U.S. 52 North in Albemarle.

restaurant eventually passed on to Lonnie's wife and then to his son, it has stayed with the old ways, producing pork barbecue that's smoky and flavorful. It is also some of the leanest barbecue you'll find anywhere. This barbecue is rather different from what's normally found in the Piedmont in that it's salty and served with a fiery sauce containing lots of ground red pepper and little, if any, sweetener or tomato ketchup. Hand-chopped with a dull cleaver that breaks the meat down into tender fibers, it's absolutely delicious.

The coarse-grated red slaw is tart, rather than sweet, and contains bits of red and green bell pepper. The hush puppies are the "shaggy dog" type—they are grainy-textured on the outside with a very fresh flavor that doesn't have too much onion or sugar. The iced tea is that most elusive of North Carolina brews—one that's not over sweetened. I found it very refreshing after the mild wallop the taste buds get from the saucy barbecue.

Whispering Pines offers burgers, sandwiches, barbecued chicken, a few dinner plates, and some homemade desserts. But, what bring the crowds in are the big servings of some of the best wood-cooked barbecue around.

BLUE MIST BARBECUE
3409 U.S. 64 East
Asheboro, N.C. 27203
336-625-3980
Breakfast, lunch, and dinner daily

Blue Mist Barbecue, which has been around since 1948, is a landmark stopping place on U.S. 64, North Carolina's mountains-to-coast highway. Old timers say that for a long time, the Blue Mist was the most popular stop between the western Piedmont and the capital. In fact, many Charlotte parents used it as a halfway point to

meet and visit with their children who were attending coll
the Raleigh-Durham-Chapel Hill area.

It's a cheerful, bustling place with an extra-long counter and lots
of booths lining the front window. There's a back dining room for
large groups and meetings. The little touches, such as a lost-dog
poster taped up beside the cash register, make you feel right at
home.

The restaurant advertises that it serves "Randolph County's only
pit-cooked barbecue." In fact, the Blue Mist has indeed remained
true to the old ways by slow-cooking pork hams and shoulders over
real coals. The place goes through around 1,500 pounds of hams
and shoulders each week to create its chopped and sliced barbecue.

On my visit, I had a sliced barbecue plate. While at some
restaurants you get a chunk of meat pulled loose with the fingers
when you order sliced barbecue, the Blue Mist served me a real
sharp-edged slice of pork. It was obviously cut from the ham
because of its extreme leanness and nearly white color. (Meat from
the pork shoulder is the dark meat of a pig, ranging in color from
gray to reddish brown. It is also suffused with tiny pockets of fat.)
The meat I was served had a readily apparent smoky flavor and was
served with a sweet-and-sour, Lexington-style sauce. Unfortunately,
it could have been more tender. Pork hams sometimes get done
faster than shoulders. As a result, they are sometimes removed from
the pit before the meat has really relaxed into its most tender stage.

Tiny hush puppies, which were a bit more firm than most,
provided an interesting balance of taste with the barbecued meat.
The plate also included white coleslaw, which was served with less
mayonnaise than most versions.

In addition to barbecue, there's a complete selection of
sandwiches, steaks, chicken, meat-and-three-vegetable combinations,
and seafood. You can also order breakfast any time of day.

I also tried one of the Blue Mist's special cheeseburgers, which
was served on a hot-grilled and slightly flattened bun. Even though

the restaurant's ground-beef patties are simply fried on a griddle, the one I sampled was cooked to perfection. The dark, crusty exterior was topped with a slice of cheese and adroitly garnished with lettuce, tomato, and mayonnaise.

I also noticed homemade persimmon pudding on the dessert menu. That's reason enough for me to swing by sometime soon and try this old favorite restaurant again.

BARBECUE INN
1341 Patton Avenue
Asheville, N.C. 28806
828-253-9615
Lunch and dinner Monday through Saturday

The late Gus Kooles, founder of Barbecue Inn, had run another restaurant in Asheville for several years when a friend suggested that he try barbecue. Gus replied that as far as he knew, barbecue was nothing but "roast pork with ketchup on it." The friend then hooked him up with an acquaintance in Goldsboro and arranged a summer visit. The idea was for Kooles to learn the secrets of preparing eastern-style barbecue and bring the delicacy back to the Asheville area. After first being mistaken for an efficiency expert by the Goldsboro restaurant employees, Kooles settled in to learn the art of cooking pork for long periods of time at low temperatures in order to make the meat tender, moist, and juicy. He came back and established Barbecue Inn in west Asheville in 1961. The place has been serving coastal-plain barbecue (among other things) to mountaineers and visitors ever since.

As a promotional stunt during the restaurant's early days, Kooles offered to give a free meal to any customer who brought him a decorative pig unlike any other he owned. The pigs arrived by the hundreds—foreign and domestic, and made from wood, metal, jade, ceramics, and other materials. Kooles ended up giving away a lot of barbecue. There are now a couple of thousand pigs arrayed on every available shelf. There are so many, in fact, that some long-time customers still refer to the Barbecue Inn as "the pig restaurant."

Second-generation family members—Woodie, Martha, and Charles Kooles—now operate the laid-back, family restaurant, which features order pads that you mark yourself. Barbecue Inn serves eastern-style barbecue moistened with their vinegar-based sauce, but the eastern tradition has been supplemented a bit, since the restaurant also prepares pork ribs, sliced and chopped beef, beef ribs, and barbecued and fried chicken. Customers usually anoint the ribs and beef barbecue with a tomato-based sauce that's sweeter than the vinegar-based version. There's Brunswick stew, as well, although Martha Kooles describes it as "a Brunswick stew of chicken." In fact, the savory chicken-and-vegetable dish more closely resembles a soup rather than a stew.

Although the backbone of the business is barbecue, Barbecue Inn has been serving Italian-style spaghetti with homemade sauce practically from the beginning, and the dish is still a favorite among many customers. The Kooles are also proud of their quarter-pound hot dogs, served with their own special chili sauce.

Barbecue Inn invites customers to finish off their meal with a free cone of ice cream from the self-service machine they've installed.

This Asheville institution is located on Patton Avenue, 2½ miles west of the French Broad River.

Bum's Restaurant

115 East Third Street
Ayden, N.C. 28513
252-746-6880
Breakfast, lunch, and dinner Monday through Saturday

At this cafeteria-style café, Latham "Bum" Dennis and his wife Shirley not only serve up terrific country-style meats and vegetables, but also offer genuine, pit-cooked pork barbecue, which is slow-roasted for hours over real wood coals.

Bum is a relative of another well-known Ayden pit master, Pete Jones, who owns the nearby Skylight Inn and is one of North Carolina's most outspoken proponents of wood-cooked barbecue. Interestingly enough, the family tradition of selling barbecue in Ayden supposedly began as early as 1830 with one of Bum's and Pete's ancestors, Skilton Dennis.

Located near Ayden's town center, Bum's is a very special place. In addition to serving some of the region's very best barbecue, the Dennises also serve North Carolina's most perfectly prepared collard greens.

This is especially impressive since Ayden promotes itself as the "Collard Capital of the World." (The town even has an annual Collard Festival, featuring both collard cooking and collard speed-eating contests.) The yellowish "cabbage collards" that seem so well suited to the sandy soil around Ayden are, to my taste, milder and sweeter than the darker green "Georgia collards" more commonly found elsewhere. Interestingly, even in this collard haven, Bum Dennis is so picky about the greens served in his restaurant that he grows them in his own garden.

Although the choices on Bum's cafeteria-style serving line change frequently, you can bet that no matter what's cooked up, it will be

Latham "Bum" Dennis and his wife Shirley of Bum's Restaurant in downtown Ayden

absolutely delicious. The pork barbecue is always available, you'll often find barbecued chicken, and there's also a wide range of other choices. Depending on the day, they may offer ham, pork chops, country-style steak, ribs, pork backbone, or fried chicken, but they also have an array of mouth-watering vegetables. The biscuits and corn bread are out of this world, as are whatever selections Bum and Shirley are serving for dessert on any given day.

As if all of this wasn't enough, the line is open for breakfast. For breakfast, you can choose from among such delights as fried ham and homemade sausage, eggs, biscuits and gravy, and pork tenderloin.

A genial man with a large handlebar moustache, Bum Dennis is well regarded in the community. He is almost always behind the counter, making his customers feel at home. Shirley is also on hand most days, and her friendly personality is one of the main reasons that the restaurant is probably one of the town's most popular gathering places. After a stop at Bum's, you'll leave not only feeling well fed but with a positive feeling about small-town life in North Carolina.

THE SKYLIGHT INN

4617 Lee Street
Ayden, N.C. 28513
752-746-4113
Lunch and dinner Monday through Saturday

"Pete" Jones, owner of the Skylight Inn in Ayden, was 72 years old at the time of the big celebration of the new millennium. He marked the occasion by observing his 65th year of being involved in the barbecue business in some form.

Pete says all he ever really wanted to do was run his own barbecue place. In 1948, at the age of 18, he was finally able to go out on his own. He followed in the footsteps of a string of relatives that traced back to Skilton Dennis, who cooked and sold barbecue in Ayden as early as 1830. During his years in the barbecue business, Pete has always stubbornly proclaimed, "If it isn't cooked with wood, it isn't barbecue," and he has been scornful of the growing trend in favor of shiny electric cookers.

Jones is also adamant that barbecue should be prepared from the whole hog, rather than just the shoulder. He's fond of saying, "The old word is, the nose is the 'barb' and the tail is the 'Q', so to have real barbecue, you have to have everything from the nose to the tail." (In fact, some people believe the word *barbecue* came from the French expression *barbe à queue*, meaning "head to tail," although scholars dismiss the theory.)

The Skylight Inn has collected numerous awards for its whole-hog barbecue, which is cooked over oak coals. In 1988, *National Geographic* recognized Pete's place as its choice for "Barbecue Capital of the World." That's when Pete went out and hired someone to build a downsized replica of the dome atop the U.S. Capitol and put it in place on his flat-roofed brick building. With a

United States flag flying proudly over the dome, the Skylight Inn is thus marked as one of the world's best spots for barbecue.

But aside from the fanciful dome and the restaurant's glass case filled with trophies, medals, plaques, and pictures of former presidents (Pete has fed several of them), this is a place that doesn't puff itself up over success or put on airs. Customers walk up to a counter to place and receive their order, then carry their food back to a table. The choices are wonderful, but limited: barbecue sandwich; barbecue tray, which comes with slaw and a piece of corn bread; and bottled soft drinks (no iced tea). There's no Brunswick stew, there are no French fries, and there are no vegetables, not even collards here in the town that calls itself the "Collard Capital of the World." For dessert, you can choose from among the packaged oatmeal cookies, honey buns, and Moon Pies displayed on a wire rack in the corner.

When you pay for your food, Pete or one of his assistants will make change from a big pile of bills and coins behind the counter, since there's no cash register. The barbecue trays are arranged as follows to insure easy carrying: a tray of chopped barbecue on the bottom, topped with a sheet of restaurant tissue, topped with a piece of flat, baked corn bread (which the Skylight serves instead of hush puppies), topped with another sheet of tissue, topped with a paper container of coleslaw and a plastic fork. It's possible to pick up the whole pile with one hand, which leaves the other hand free to hold your bottled drink as you shuffle carefully back to your table.

What's really important here, though, is that Pete Jones serves some of the most flavorful, pit-cooked barbecue on the earth. That's because of the slow wood-cooking, to be sure, but it's also because he doesn't mind chopping a fair amount of the fat and crispy "cracklings" in with the lean meat pulled from the cooked pig. In any dish, the fat always carries the flavor, which is why we sautée onions or garlic in olive oil or butter. In barbecue, a slightly higher fat content means a big increase in flavor. Seasoned simply with salt and Texas Pete hot sauce while it's being chopped, the meat is so tender, soft, and luxuriant on the tongue that it really doesn't need any of the Skylight Inn's eastern-style sauce.

Pete's barbecue may be even more of a threat to our cholesterol levels than most, but enjoyed in moderation, it's an incredible treat. Since the world has literally beaten a path to the door of this humble establishment, it's a place you definitely don't want to miss.

Sid's Catering
455 South Railroad Avenue
Beulaville, N.C. 28518
910-298-3549
Saturdays only from 9:30 until...

Sid's is another of those great little places you'd never know about unless you lived in or near the town of Beulaville. Of course, someone could tell you about it, which is how I got the tip.

This combination restaurant, takeout kitchen, and catering service is housed in a large wooden building that's considerably nicer than the quarters occupied by many barbecue places. You would never know it was there unless—well, unless you *already* knew it was there. It sits completely hidden behind an ordinary brick, ranch-style home on the outskirts of Beulaville in Duplin County. You actually have to turn into the driveway and drive completely past the house before you even catch sight of the place. I drove past three times.

All of the cooking is done by Sid Blizzard Sr. and Sid Blizzard Jr.

Ann and Sid Blizzard and Sid Junior cater and run a Saturday-only restaurant/ takeout in Beulaville.

Sid Sr.'s wife Ann also lends a major helping hand. Since the takeout and restaurant business operates only on Saturday, Sid Jr. is able to pursue his vocation as a full-time schoolteacher and still follow in the footsteps of his father. A former farmer, Sid Sr. first began selling his own home-cooked barbecue out of the back of a camper in 1977. The business was so successful that the elder Blizzards built a small cookhouse behind their home. After Hurricane Fran damaged the cookhouse, they enlarged the facility.

Whole-hog pork barbecue and barbecued chicken are the mainstays of the Blizzards' menu. Since I didn't arrive until after 1:00 P.M. on Saturday, all the barbecued chicken had already been sold. I was told by several people that it's awesome stuff—slow cooked over coals and served without sauce, which can be added later according to taste. I did, however, enjoy a plate of nearly perfect, eastern-style barbecue, served with a mild vinegar sauce.

The business is called Sid's Catering because the lion's share of the business comes from serving group functions. In fact, Sid's was preparing to serve a group of ninety the day after I visited. Next to catering, the bulk of the business comes from the takeout trade. In small towns in North Carolina that have weekend-only barbecue stands, it seems eating barbecue and fixin's for the noon meal on Saturday is a tradition for many families. Indeed, on Saturday mornings in Beulaville, the phone at Sid's rings steadily. It seems that half the town's residents find their way up the circular driveway and dash inside to claim their takeout orders.

If you're planning a visit, be sure to arrive early enough to enjoy both the pork *and* the chicken!

From downtown Beulaville, turn west on N.C. 24, heading towards Kenansville. Turn left on South Railroad Avenue and go 0.3 mile to 455 South Railroad Avenue, which is on the left. The restaurant is hidden behind the brick house.

The Woodlands Barbecue & Pickin' Parlor
8304 U.S. 321 Bypass
Blowing Rock, N.C. 28605
828-295-3651
Lunch and dinner Tuesday through Sunday

The word "pickin' " in this restaurant's name refers to what musicians do here with banjos and guitars every Saturday night, rather than what the guests do at a whole-hog barbecue in the coastal plain. After all, this is western North Carolina, where the custom of slow-cooking barbecue never really caught on until fairly recently. Even then it was primarily practiced as a way to attract and feed tourists. For decades, when mountaineers got ready to

The Woodlands Barbecue & Pickin' Parlor in Blowing Rock

slaughter hogs, they thought primarily in terms of making sausage and curing country hams.

That being said, Woodlands should definitely be rated the best barbecue place in the North Carolina mountains. While the beef brisket and pork ribs at Woodlands may be influenced by establishments west of North Carolina, the chopped pork qualifies not only as authentic North Carolina barbecue, but as doggone *good* North Carolina barbecue.

In 1991, a fire did extensive damage to the original location, but the owners rebuilt on the same spot without losing their customers' loyalty. Like a lot of places in the mountains, Woodlands' new building is a mixture of Bavarian *kitsch* and hillbilly humor. There are wooden floors, rough-wood paneling, picnic tables and benches, and lots of cutesy pig pictures and figures. There is even a send-up of the Mona Lisa featuring Miss Piggy. In addition to the barbecue, the menu also includes some Mexican dishes and a few sandwiches.

19

Woodlands features chopped and sliced Boston butts; chopped beef; turkey; chicken; and pork ribs. All are cooked in a Southern Pride™ cooker. To envision the cooker, picture a small Ferris wheel with racks of meat, instead of seats, turning slowly in an oven-like chamber full of wood smoke.

The coarse hand-chopped pork is lean yet juicy. It has an appealing smoke flavor and color, plus a generous sprinkling of pieces of crispy outside-brown meat. Two choices of sauce are available: a fiery vinegar blend labeled "hot" and a Lexington-style dip labeled "mild."

My plate was served with an excellent barbecue slaw (white slaw is also available), a small piece of grilled corn-on-the-cob, baked beans, and a choice of either hot or mild corn bread. I ordered the hot, but found it to have neither a warm-enough temperature nor a spicy-enough taste to suit me.

I also sampled the chicken and ribs, both of which are cooked in the rotating Southern Pride™ device for a couple of hours less than the pork butts and the beef. In my opinion, both the chicken and the ribs could have been cooked for a longer period of time, perhaps at a lower temperature, since both were a bit on the firm side. I like my chicken and ribs cooked until they reach that tender, relaxed stage at which the meat is almost ready to pull loose from the bone. However, both the chicken and the ribs had an excellent, smoky flavor and were served with a tasty sauce.

Although Woodlands is far from the heart of barbecue country, the college students from Appalachian State University in nearby Boone, skiers, and summer tourists in the Blowing Rock vicinity seem to keep the spacious upstairs and downstairs dining rooms at Woodlands busy just about year-round.

Carolina BBQ & Seafood is a wood-burner on Burlington's Maple Avenue.

CAROLINA BBQ & SEAFOOD

1540 Maple Avenue
Burlington, N.C. 27215
336-227-0976
Lunch and dinner Monday through Saturday

Carolina BBQ & Seafood is located on Burlington's Maple Avenue, in a section that once was one of the town's several mill neighborhoods. Housed in a small, frame building with a modest gravel parking lot, it's definitely a blue-collar type of place. However, there's one feature that places it on a plane with, if not above, the most upscale barbecue restaurants: a dump-truck load of real wood out back. Like Stamey's, its larger and better-known counterpart in Greensboro, the restaurant pit-cooks with the coals of what appear to be wood scraps from a furniture plant. Believe me, these scraps flavor barbecue every bit as well as split hardwood logs or slabs.

Inside, you'll find lots of old western-movie posters on the walls, a collection of ceramic pigs in a glass case in front of the cash register, and a menu that offers barbecued pork shoulders, seafood, sandwiches, fried chicken, and hamburger steaks with onions.

Barbecue is available chopped and sliced. Either way, it's tender and has a rich smoky flavor. The portions are very generous, whether on a sandwich or on a plate. The sandwich is piled so high it's hard to bite into. White slaw, rather than the red barbecue variety, is the norm here, as it is throughout this transitional area between the east and Piedmont. The small, tasty hush puppies have exteriors that resemble rough tree bark.

Personally, I find the sauce here undistinguished, with too little "tang" and too much bland tomato flavor. For that reason, I tend to order my barbecue without sauce. For some strange reason, this always seems to confuse the help at the takeout window. They usually have to prepare my order twice, since the first order arrives *with* sauce. Ah, well, we're nitpicking now. The barbecue itself is terrific enough that such small details should be excused.

Unless you're in the mood for adventure, I wouldn't come here especially for Brunswick stew, which resembles Dinty Moore beef stew. It also contains the inauthentic ingredients of okra and green peas. I suppose if a good number of customers didn't like it, they wouldn't keep it on the menu, so what do I know?

Although this place seems very popular with an established local crowd, not too many out-of-towners appear to know about it yet. Since it's within two or three miles of Interstate 85, more people should take a detour and give it a try.

To reach Carolina BBQ & Seafood, take Exit 145 (N.C. 49) and turn toward Burlington. The restaurant is 0.9 mile on the right, before you reach the downtown district.

HUEY'S BARBECUE
3523 South Church Street
Burlington, N.C. 27215
336-586-0880
Lunch and dinner Monday through Saturday

Huey's Barbecue is housed in a narrow storefront in the Westbrook Shopping Center, which is located between Burlington and Elon. The interior re-creates the feel of a 1950s soda shop. Over the door, you'll see a sign with *BBQ* in big letters. Right below that, there's another sign that reads: "Don't shop hungry—grab a quick hot dog now." With the latter pronouncement, some customers may not walk in brimming with confidence about the barbecue.

Actually, it's not bad, and the hot dogs are pretty good, too. The 'cue comes very finely chopped and served on a plate, on a regular sandwich, or on a large sandwich known as "The Boss Hog." It's difficult to characterize the barbecue as either eastern- or Lexington-style, since it's topped with white slaw and tastes premoistened with eastern-style vinegar. The problem is that it is topped with another sauce that's thicker and redder than just about any I've seen. Surprisingly, the tomato-based sauce also has a real vinegar tang to it. Somehow, all these elements manage to go together and form a sandwich that's easy on the taste buds.

The owner must be appealing to a lot of the *right* taste buds, since Huey's is the official barbecue caterer for all the Elon University athletic events. This means the owner and his crew are frequently under a tent at ball games, serving barbecue to big contributors. Any of these powerful Elon supporters could probably have him replaced in a heartbeat if they didn't like his barbecue.

Huey's all-beef hot dogs are cooked on the grill, rather than boiled. This cooks some of the moisture out of them and makes them more chewy and salty than they would be otherwise. A sweet chili sauce provides a nice balance.

During the fall and winter months, Huey's has an unusual stew, which contains the normal ingredients for Brunswick stew plus black-eyed peas. The first time I saw this concoction I scoffed, but after trying a few bowls of it, I find that it's growing on me. However, I'm not sure I'm ready to refer to it as *Brunswick* stew.

To finish off a meal, Huey's serves hand-dipped Breyer's Ice Cream and makes its own meringue-topped lemon-icebox and chocolate pies.

Huey's is a good, safe bet for when you find yourself on U.S. 70 east of Burlington and really need some barbecue right away. If you're an Elon athletic backer, of course, the barbecue from Huey's is food for the gods.

HURSEY'S BAR-B-Q
1834 South Church Street
Burlington, N.C. 27215
336-226-1694
Lunch and dinner Monday through Saturday

The Hursey family restaurant is a simple, rustic brick structure situated on the busy corner of U.S. 70 and N.C. 62 near downtown Burlington. Chuck and Chris, owner Charles Hursey's sons, cook virtually all the restaurant's barbecue on their two wood-burning pits. The pits are situated so that, on the three days each week when Hursey's normally cooks its barbecue, clouds of smoke, deliciously redolent of roasting pork shoulders, roll across the busy traffic

Hursey's Bar-B-Q on Church Street (U.S. 70) in Burlington

ways, mesmerizing the drivers and causing many of them to pull into the restaurant's parking lot.

Inside, near the takeout counter, plaques and framed write-ups testify to the Hurseys having won several important barbecue contests, cook-offs, readers' choice polls, and to their having served their barbecue to former presidents Bill Clinton and George Bush Sr.

It's true that Hursey's has an electric pit, as well, but Chuck Hursey says it's mostly used for ribs, which are not a mainstay on the menu. Chuck says that on very rare occasions when he gets overwhelmingly busy or has a larger-than-normal catering job, he'll mix one batch of chopped pork from the electric cooker (18 shoulders maximum) with a full batch of meat from the two wood-burning pits (60 shoulders), which is a three-to-one ratio of wood-cooked to electric-cooked meat. That's smoky enough to satisfy all but the pickiest palates.

Some people may get confused about the question of pit cooking at the restaurant, since Charles Hursey also owns and operates a well-known wholesale operation outside Burlington that *does* cook all its meat in electric pits. Chuck Hursey says practically none of that meat is ever served at the Church Street restaurant.

Despite the reference to *pig pickin'* emblazoned on the signs, catering trucks, and menus, pork shoulders rather than whole hogs

25

are cooked here. Hursey's barbecue is pleasantly smoky, mild, and tender. The chopped meat is minced by machine to a consistency that's a little too fine and a little dry for my personal taste, but the pulled hunks of pork that Hursey calls "pig pickin' style" are always moist and tasty, with a very nice texture on the teeth and tongue. His sauce, the recipe for which was reportedly won by his father in a poker game, is a mild blend with both vinegar and tomato overtones, plus a bit of sweetener, and it's very popular in the area.

Members of the warm, friendly Hursey family treat everyone with respect and help to create a very inviting atmosphere in the restaurant. Unless a barbecue seeker is dead set on seeing and smelling the wood-burning pit in action on a given day, he or she will have an enjoyable meal here, as well as a pleasant time getting to know the Hursey family.

DANNY'S BAR-B-QUE
311 Asheville Avenue
Cary, N.C. 27511
919-851-5541
Lunch and dinner Monday through Saturday

Second location:
2845 Miami Boulevard (at its intersection with Alexander Avenue)
Durham, NC 27705
Lunch only Monday through Saturday

Let's acknowledge right up front that this is basically Texas-style barbecue, brought to Wake County by way of the Jacksonville, Florida, area where the owner of Danny's Bar-B-Que lived with his family before moving to Cary in 1989. A note in the menu says that after their arrival, the family went in search of the barbecue they were used to, "real pit, hickory smoked BBQ," but could find only "shredded pork with vinegar sauce." Hence, Danny's Bar-B-Que came into being, serving pork, pork ribs (spareribs and baby backs), chicken, and beef cooked in an electric smoker (with some hickory wood added).

First of all, Danny's family probably *did* have trouble finding traditional, pit-cooked North Carolina barbecue in the capital-city area, since there are only a couple of places in the immediate vicinity still cooking over live coals. We have settled for what I call "generic" barbecue, flavored only by the sauce (and often with little flavor at all) for so long in the eastern portion of the state that we should be willing to accept a fair criticism.

However, had Danny's family ventured just a short distance to the west (say to Allen & Son in Chapel Hill), they would have discovered the first of many places stretching on to the west that cook over a *real* hickory or oak pit, not its modern-day, electric-smoking counterpart, which is probably what *they* settled for back home in Jacksonville. Let's give them a "C-minus" for incomplete research.

Danny's really packs in the crowds at his place (I had a 20-minute wait the day I was there), and the viewers of WRAL-TV voted his barbecue "Best in Wake County" in 1997, so the restaurant should be given its due respect. On the other hand, it's probably only because he moved to an area so relatively lacking in the *best* North Carolina barbecue that he's in business at all, a circumstance that probably explains the award, too.

All kidding aside, I've enjoyed every meal I've ever had at Danny's, and I've had several. I find that his meats, which are served without sauce, are lean, pleasantly smoke-ringed and smoke-flavored, and tasty. The sauces, offered on the side, include a dark, thick, molasses-flavored number; a thick, mustard-based,

Carolina-inspired sauce; a spicy-hot, thick sauce that's reddish-orange in color; and a weak version of eastern-style sauce that needs more pepper.

The pork at Danny's doesn't quite have the same falling-apart tenderness and juiciness that results when whole shoulders or butts (the upper half of the shoulder) are cooked extremely slowly. The pinkish color and flavor that come from merely *smoking* meat is also different from when the meat is both smoked *and* grilled by being cooked directly over live coals. That's because, in the former case, it's missing the unique flavor that only comes from fat dripping onto hot coals, which produces an aromatic steam that envelopes the meat. Academic discussions aside, Danny's barbecued meats and well-prepared side dishes offer a refreshing change-of-pace, yet provide an experience that's not totally off the reservation in terms of what we all enjoy about North Carolina's best barbecue. The ambiance at Danny's clean, modern facility isn't the same as it would be at some dilapidated barbecue shack out in the country, more's the pity, but the atmosphere *is* friendly and Danny deserves for all of us to go by and give him a pat on the back for having sense enough to move to North Carolina.

ALLEN & SON BAR-B-Q

10/1/05

6203 Millhouse Road (at N.C. 86)
Chapel Hill, N.C. 27516
919-942-7576
Lunch and dinner Monday through Saturday

You might say that Allen & Son Bar-B-Q on N.C. 86, north of

Chapel Hill, is as much a craftsman's gallery or an artist's studio as it is a barbecue joint. It's here that the traditional craft—indeed the *art*—of barbecue is practiced and maintained with single-minded dedication by the owner, Keith Allen.

In an age when hardwood is increasingly expensive and hard to find, and when some of the state's most prominent barbecue experts are turning to gas or electric cookers to save time and labor, Allen continues to scour the state to find the hickory he insists on for his pits. And once hickory logs the size of tree trunks are delivered to his property, Allen himself cuts and splits the logs by hand, using a chain saw, sledge hammer, and maul.

When the mahogany-hued shoulders are removed from the smoky pits, Allen is most often the one who pulls the meat cleanly from the bones, then, with a cleaver in each hand, chops it into barbecue in an unceasing rhythm.

This is barbecue that's unlike anything else you'll experience in North Carolina. Pure-hickory coals, burned down from seasoned wood, are scattered periodically beneath the roasting shoulders. They give the meat a dark, hard-edged robust flavor without making it overly smoky. The falling-apart-tender shreds of lean pork are sown heavily with bits of the chewy, dark "outside brown." Allen's burgundy-colored, peppery sauce, which contains no tomato, has enough fat in it to glaze the barbecue and smooth out the tartness of the liquid on the tongue.

The restaurant also makes delicious homemade French fries, sliced from long potatoes with the skins mostly intact and fried a shade darker than might be expected. Along with the hearty, delicious Brunswick stew, which is perhaps the best I've ever tasted in the Piedmont, the French fries enhance the flavor of the hickory-cooked barbecue to perfection. Allen's baked beans also complement the chopped pork nicely.

Finally, Allen & Son goes far beyond the ordinary in its offerings of outstanding homemade desserts. Selections include pecan pie

Allen & Son Bar-B-Q cooks over pure hickory just off N.C. 86 north of Chapel Hill.

with homemade ice cream, cream-cheese pound cake, blueberry pie, and rich, thick bread pudding with lots of plump raisins.

Allen & Son's modest exterior and simple dining room give little hint of what is in store for the first-time customer who loves real barbecue. However, after experiencing the products of Allen's talent once, a patron is likely to do almost anything in order to return.

To reach Allen & Son, take N.C. 86 off Interstate 40 and head north toward Hillsborough. Allen & Son is located on the left at Millhouse Road. If you reach the railroad tracks, you've gone too far.

BUBBA'S BARBECUE
4400 Sunset Road
Charlotte, N.C. 28216
704-393-2000
Lunch and dinner daily

When banker-turned-restaurateur Ralph Miller bought the venerable Spoon's Barbecue on Charlotte's South Boulevard in 1986, he changed the name to Bubba's not long afterwards. In 1994, Miller moved Bubba's to the present location on Sunset Road, just off Interstate 77, north of Charlotte. (After the move, the original owner of Spoon's came out of retirement and now operates the lunchtime-only "*Bill* Spoon's Barbecue" at the original South Boulevard location.) The marketing approach employed by Miller, first at Spoon's and now at Bubba's, is offering whole-hog, eastern-style barbecue in a city where the Lexington version is dominant.

Bubba's is located in a new, one-story frame building, decorated inside by cheerful, yellow-checked tablecloths and a big red-and-white "Bubba's Barbecue" sign. Outside, there are two stationary pigs and a sign reading, "Pig Rides—Thousands of Miles an Hour," referring of course to the speed of the earth as it moves through space.

That same sort of literary license applies to the menu at Bubba's, which advertises whole-hog barbecue "slow-cooked for over ten hours using hickory wood." Actually there's no evidence of an old-fashioned pit or a woodpile at Bubba's, and the whole pigs are cooked in two electric pits, with a little hickory wood added during the last two hours.

As you might expect, the barbecue at Bubba's is finely chopped and has little smoky taste. But, we have to admit that those characteristics put Miller's product right in line with how *most* eastern-style barbecue could be described these days. This is good, average, middle-of-the-pack eastern barbecue, and while it isn't *distinguished* barbecue, it certainly satisfies your everyday need for a pig fix. The house sauce is a typical vinegar-based mixture, while an alternative sauce for chicken and ribs is thicker and sweeter and has a touch of liquid smoke added. The slaw is the yellow eastern variety. There is also Brunswick stew available to accompany the chopped pork (and to make any eastern fan's heart glad), and the Luzianne iced tea is extremely tasty.

Besides whole-hog barbecue, Bubba's offers ribs, barbecued chicken, chicken and dumplings, sandwiches, and some plate specials, including meat loaf and beef tips and rice.

While Bubba's isn't the slightest bit fancy or unique, it is a pretty good place to do exactly what its slogan recommends: "pig out with the locals."

HOG HEAVEN BAR-B-Q

1600 Purser Drive
Charlotte, N.C. 28215
705-534-0514
Lunch only Monday and Tuesday
Lunch and dinner Wednesday through Saturday

Hog Heaven may be located in an out-of-the-way spot, but it's the home of the best Lexington-style barbecue in Charlotte. You'll find Hog Heaven just off the intersection of Eastway Drive and Sugar Creek Road, near Garinger High School. The restaurant's logo of a pig in a chef's hat resting on a cloud with a rainbow behind him may be a bit of a reach in terms of the bliss you'll experience at Hog Heaven. However, I recommend this spot for those who need a Lexington-style barbecue fix and don't have time to drive north to Davidson County to get it.

On the front side of the modest, little gray building with bright blue awnings is an unpainted wooden deck with picnic tables. Inside, what atmosphere exists in the six-booth dining room comes from NASCAR prints and whatever's playing on the TV set. The sink where customers can wash their hands is located in a hallway between the counter and the kitchen area.

At one time, the large brick pits burned wood, but they've been converted to gas for at least a decade. (The restaurant was founded in 1982.) Nevertheless, Hog Heaven's chopped and sliced pork barbecue is quite tasty. The fairly finely chopped barbecue admittedly has no discernable wood flavor, but it's very well seasoned and is quite moistened by an excellent Lexington-style dip. Savory barbecue beans and a delicious, chunky-textured barbecue slaw complement the chopped pork extremely well. You can also order the delicious and authentic Brunswick stew, which is prepared according to a family recipe brought from Creedmoor by owner Sonny Lyon. The iced tea is a flavorful, well-balanced brew that's perfect for those of us who enjoy sweet tea but prefer that the sugar be added with a delicate touch.

In addition to everything else, you'll find pork ribs, barbecued chicken, and excellent hot dogs with homemade chili.

To top it all off, you should try some of the superb homemade coconut pie made by Sonny's wife.

OLD HICKORY HOUSE RESTAURANT

6538 North Tryon Street
Charlotte, N.C. 28213
704-596-8014
Lunch and dinner Monday through Saturday

Having been in business since 1956, this restaurant is a real Charlotte landmark. However, the location on North Tryon, just a couple of miles south of Harris Boulevard, makes it somewhat out of the way for most people these days. On the outside, at least, the building isn't all that inviting.

Inside, however, the restaurant is warm and attractive, with wagon-wheel light fixtures, mounted with replicas of kerosene lamps. Large cuts of meat are kept on a small, wood-burning pit behind the counter, where they sizzle and hiss, creating smoke and sending tantalizing smells wafting throughout the room. Chances are, the meat that's actually being served is kept wrapped in aluminum foil back in the kitchen to keep it from drying out.

We should make it clear that while the Old Hickory House specializes in pit-cooked barbecue and Brunswick stew, it isn't exactly the North Carolina-style barbecue or the stew which most of us have come to expect. Instead, the menu here has distinct Georgia and Alabama roots, with recipes brought to Charlotte in the mid-1950s by the Carter family, who still run the place today.

The chopped pork at the Old Hickory House is delicious, with lots of crusty brown-outside meat, a reddish hue from the pit, and a good, strong smoky flavor. Served hot in a ramekin, the thick, red sauce is definitely more of a Memphis- or Texas-style sauce than a Lexington dip. It's still very appealing, with a good deal of onion flavor and little bits of barbecued meat mixed in. The white coleslaw is quite good and not all that different from the North

Carolina norm, except that it contains bits of dill, rather than sweet, pickle. Crispy, round hush puppies have lots of onion and complement the crusty, smoky pork very well.

Darker and more robust, certainly, than the typical eastern Carolina Brunswick stew, the Old Hickory House version of this dish is intriguing. It contains a lot of pepper and has no baby lima beans, which have been an ingredient in every Brunswick stew I had ever tasted before trying this recipe. Despite those differences, however, the stew was so tasty and so different that I bought a quart to take home. As I enjoyed it during the next several days, I struggled to identify another ingredient that had to do more with giving the stew a smooth, thick texture than with the taste itself. It finally came to me that what this stew contained was stale bread, which pretty well dissolves in the hot liquid but which thickens the stew and makes it very smooth and pleasant on the tongue. Ironically, Brunswick stew is said to have begun in Brunswick County, Virginia, in the early 1800s, and the original version is said to have contained squirrel meat, onions, and—you guessed it— stale bread. The Old Hickory House Brunswick stew may be a lot closer to the original than our modern-day North Carolina version, which ordinarily contains chicken, pork, tomatoes, lima beans, corn, onions, and seasonings. No matter how much of a purist you may be about Brunswick stew, I recommend that you put aside your preconceptions and give this a try, because it's very, very good.

Even though it's grounded in a slightly different tradition, The Old Hickory House definitely belongs in any comprehensive listing of top North Carolina barbecue places.

GARY'S BARBECUE

620 U.S. 29 North
China Grove, N.C. 28023
704-857-8314
Lunch and dinner Monday through Saturday

Growing up in China Grove, Gary Ritchie always wanted to own a barbecue place. In 1971, he opened Gary's Barbecue in a renovated service station and garage. Today, the parking lot is nearly always full. Inside, warm wood paneling, cheerful yellow booths, and a colorful collection of thousands of cigarette advertisements and soft-drink signs, the majority of which are for Coke and Pepsi, help create a really homey, inviting atmosphere.

At one time, Gary's Barbecue pit-cooked its pork-shoulder barbecue over wood coals. A long time after he switched from the old-fashioned pits to electric cookers, Ritchie kept a pile of wood outside just for appearances. The wood turned so gray and weathered that it wasn't fooling anybody, so the decorative pile of split logs is no longer there.

But people's memories are incredibly powerful. Even though today's chopped barbecue at Gary's is, in my opinion, merely average by any measure, there are many present and former area residents who believe it is now and always has been the best barbecue they've ever eaten. Who's to say they're wrong? Even though China Grove is on the western side of the North Carolina Piedmont, one former resident gushed, "There's nothing like eastern Carolina barbecue, and no place like Gary's to get it!"

At least, I can say that Gary's barbecue is lean and not too finely chopped. It's served with the hotter version of Piedmont dip characteristic of Rowan County. You also get red barbecue slaw, which is a bit more tart than the usual Lexington-style slaw, and loose, grainy hush puppies.

The atmosphere at Gary's *is* inviting and conducive to forming pleasant memories, and that's obviously been Ritchie's chief gift to the community. I readily admit that the taste of the barbecue is small potatoes by comparison.

KEATON'S BBQ
17365 Cool Springs Road
Cleveland, N.C. 27013
704-278-1619
Lunch and dinner Wednesday through Saturday

Halfway between Mocksville and Statesville is a wonderful, rural hole in the wall, where the pork barbecue takes a backseat to the barbecued chicken. Here the chicken isn't actually barbecued but deep-fried, then immersed in a memorable, mysterious barbecue sauce. No matter. Keaton's is an absolute must-stop. If the restaurant's mention here or the glowing write-up in the January 2002 issue of *Gourmet* isn't enough to convince you, then maybe the guest book signed by visitors from all over the world will be.

The late B.W. Keaton began the business as a neighborhood grill in 1953. A portrait hanging on the wall shows a large, jovial-looking black gentleman dressed in an apron, with a cigarette dangling from his lips. The original place had a cement floor inside and wood-burning barbecue pits outside. Unlike most barbecue places, it served beer, just as it does today, but Keaton kept his place from turning into a typical beer joint by insisting that his patrons behave themselves. To this day, signs warning against loud talking or the use of profanity are displayed prominently.

Along with pit cooking his pork, Keaton experimented with unique ways to prepare chicken. Developing just the right sauce took quite awhile. Keaton said later that the dogs ended up eating a lot of his chicken during the trial-and-error period. He finally came up with the right recipe when he cooked half and whole chickens in a deep-fat fryer and then dipped them in either a mild or spicy barbecue sauce for a few seconds. Once the sauces were perfected, Keaton's business soared. He was quoted as saying there was now little left for the dogs but clean-picked bones. But Keaton always kept his sauce recipes a secret. Not long before his death, he even turned down $10,000 rather than divulge their contents.

Today, Kathleen Murray, B.W. Keaton's niece, runs the restaurant. The original modest barbecue pit and chicken shack have expanded. Although the premises now include a plain dining room, customers still line up at the counter to order and pay before going to a numbered booth to await the arrival of their order. Other than the half and whole chickens, the only items on the menu are barbecued pork sandwiches; side dishes of beans, coleslaw, and macaroni and cheese; desserts such as banana pudding and Cherry Yum-Yum; and beverages. A customer standing next to me in line recognized me from television and was so delighted that I intended to write about the place that he insisted on buying my entire dinner.

I ordered a barbecue sandwich for research purposes, and I found it to be moderately good. The electric-pit-cooked pork was chopped fine and mixed liberally with a sweet sauce. My attention was soon drawn, though, to the absolutely tantalizing aroma of the half chicken. Its crisp skin gradually softens after the split bird is immersed in a dark, spicy sauce. As I expected, the chicken was moist and bursting with a superb flavor that, as one customer had described it, "penetrated all the way to the bone." A serving of rich, chewy macaroni and cheese and a half-pitcher of excellent iced tea accompanied the world-class chicken.

Although miles of orderly, western Piedmont farmland surround the restaurant, you can reach Keaton's easily from Interstate 40. Between Mocksville and Statesville, take Exit 162 (Cool Springs) and turn west on to U.S. 64. After passing a Texaco station on the left and crossing a narrow bridge, turn left on to Woodleaf Road, which turns into Cool Springs Road. The restaurant is located on the right, approximately two to three miles from the intersection of Woodleaf Road and U.S. 64. Be sure to sign the guest book and remember: no loud talking or profanity!

BOB'S BARBECUE
1589 N.C. 56
Creedmoor, N.C. 27522
919-528-2081
Lunch and dinner Monday through Saturday

Bob's Barbecue was built in 1970, before Interstate 85 came through just a couple of hundred yards away and before the area around Creedmoor's Exit 191 experienced a mushrooming growth of motels, shopping centers, and fast-food places. Between the interstate boom and the rapid growth of nearby Butner, Bob's Barbecue has operated at a wide-open pace for years. Over those years, it has built a reputation for good, middle-of-the-road barbecue, which is really neither eastern- nor Lexington-style.

The busy restaurant has always had to turn out good food quickly, so it operates with a mini-cafeteria line. Orders for barbecue and side dishes are filled on the spot, while orders for hamburgers, seafood, and other selections are sent back to the kitchen and then brought to the table.

The barbecue at Bob's comes from pork shoulders cooked on an electric pit, and the meat is incredibly lean, without a trace of skin or fat. The sauce is a mild, sweet mixture that—like the town of Creedmoor—straddles the fence between coastal plain and Piedmont. Consistency, rather than excitement, characterizes this barbecue. Since people like to know what to expect, locals and Interstate 85 travelers alike have indicated their satisfaction by bringing in a steadily increasing business.

Brunswick stew is a big specialty at Bob's, where it's cooked four or five days a week, 40 gallons at a time. The first thing customers coming through the line see is a big pot of stew, sitting in a pan of simmering water, ready to be served.

Another perennial favorite is Bob's homemade chicken salad, served not only at the restaurant, but also at wedding receptions and parties throughout the region.

If there's just one thing about Bob's that really stands out in people's minds even above the barbecue, it's the irresistible homemade pies. Forty or fifty are made and sold every day, including chocolate-cream, chocolate-chess, and sweet-potato, with the latter being far and away the most popular.

To reach Bob's Barbecue, drive twelve miles north of Durham on Interstate 85. Take Exit 191 (Butner-Creedmoor) and turn east toward Creedmoor on N.C. 56. The restaurant is on the left, 100 yards from the interchange.

TROUTMAN'S BARBECUE

18466 South N.C. 109
Denton, N.C. 27239
336-859-2206
Lunch and dinner Monday through Saturday
Curb service offered

This southeastern Davidson County community is home to the annual Old Time Thresher's Reunion, a festival celebrating farm machinery of bygone years. Its second claim to fame could well be Troutman's Barbecue on N.C. 109, one of the two main thoroughfares through town.

There are three other Troutman's over in Cabarrus County, but there's no business connection between the owner of those establishments and Jimmy Troutman, the self-proclaimed "boss hog" of the Denton restaurant. For my money, this Troutman's is the best. Jimmy obviously thinks so too, since he's bold enough to claim that he serves "the best barbecue in the world."

I don't know if it's the world's best, but it's certainly very, very good. You know you're in for a genuine barbecue experience the minute you drive up to the cinder-block building. Behind the modest building, which is veneered in front by a layer of brick, you'll see three big pit chimneys and a big woodpile. Inside, you'll find two plain, sheet-paneled dining rooms and a few counter stools. The menus have a religious message printed on the front, which tells you that this place is run by no-nonsense, heart-of-the-matter folks—an impression that's confirmed when you read on the menu that Troutman's still cooks its barbecue over wood coals every day.

And—and this is a *big* and—like nearly all the really good barbecue restaurants, Troutman's still offers curb service.

The moist, tender chopped 'cue has a wonderful, robust, wood-cooked flavor and lots of chewy bits of "outside brown" meat from the surface of the pork shoulder. Troutman's sauce is thicker than the typical Lexington-style dip. As a result, it tends to sit atop the chopped meat like sauce on spaghetti rather than soaking into the barbecue. Personally, I would thin the sauce down just a bit. But hey, there's no reason to tamper with success, and lots of people are obviously very fond of it just the way it is. The barbecue is served with savory, fresh-tasting hush puppies and Troutman's signature barbecue slaw. The slaw here is a chunkier-than-normal side dish that's sold in containers in area groceries and is some of the best slaw I've ever tasted. You can finish off the meal with an absolutely enormous bowl of homemade banana pudding, topped with whipped cream, rather than the more commonly found egg-white and sugar meringue. For dessert, you can also choose homemade peach cobbler or strawberry cobbler, when the strawberries are in season.

Next time you're in the vicinity of Lexington, Asheboro, or High Point, drive the 15-20 extra miles to Denton and check out Troutman's. It's right on N.C. 109.

GRADY'S BARBECUE
Arrington Bridge Road and Sleepy Creek Road
Dudley, N.C. 28333
919-735-7243
Breakfast and lunch Monday through Friday
Breakfast, lunch, and dinner until 6:00 P.M. on Saturday

Put on a tape of the Coasters' oldie, "Searchin' " as you set out across the countryside south of Goldsboro on a truly adventurous search for this jewel of a place. You'll need to check your turns and distances carefully, but you'll also enjoy some beautiful rural countryside. You'll probably pick up an evocative aroma of roasting pork and see a haze of blue-white smoke emanating from the barbecue pits first. Then between the arms of two seemingly lonesome rural roads, you'll come upon a small, nondescript, white-painted building with the pits out back. The crossroads only seem lonesome for a moment, as you realize that there's actually quite a bit of local traffic. Nearly all of it is turning into Grady's, which is pronounced "Graddy's."

Quite simply, Grady's is one of the best-kept secrets in North Carolina.

Gerri and Stephen Grady of Grady's Barbecue run a wood-burner near Goldsboro.

Of course, the locals all know about it and are probably involved in a good-natured conspiracy to keep the rest of us from finding out too much. They don't want outsiders to overwhelm the place. In fact, this place really is so far off the beaten track that there's practically no chance that the average barbecue lover would ever stumble across it. However, if you're armed with directions and in the mood for a pleasant, cross-country mission, you will be rewarded with some of the best pit-cooked barbecue in eastern North Carolina, if not the entire state.

Stephen Grady, a quiet, dignified black gentleman, opened the place in 1986. Grady worked for a sawmill at the time. Since the mill owner promised all the wood he could use for free, Grady thought he saw a great opportunity to build a business for his wife Gerri to run. He says he figured he could get the hogs on the fire early each morning, then turn things over to Gerri while he went off to saw lumber for the rest of the day. Well, Stephen Grady left the sawmill several years ago. He found that the barbecue business, including a good bit of catering, was enough to keep both him and Gerri busy full time.

Grady's serves absolutely superb wood-cooked, whole-hog barbecue in a tiny dining room that seats no more than twenty. The tender, delectable meat has a subtle, but unmistakable, wood-smoke taste. It is attractively laced with bits of crispy, tasty skin and is moistened by a well-mannered vinegar-based sauce that does contain some sugar. Simple boiled potatoes and sweet, white coleslaw complement the barbecue perfectly, as do large hush puppies that are light, crispy, and not overly sweet. The place also serves top-notch, robust iced tea.

Grady's offers other hearty daily specials. I sampled country-style cabbage, black-eyed peas, and a wonderful hamburger steak with gravy. They also offer a variety of sandwiches. Grady's opens early for breakfast every day but Sunday. Local residents arrive in a steady stream throughout the day for takeout orders.

An article in the November 2000 issue of GQ magazine gives Grady's its "Best Barbecue" rating, proving that excellence will generally make itself known even if it's practiced at an out-of-the-way rural North Carolina crossroad. At your earliest convenience, plan a trip to meet Stephen and his cheery, outgoing wife Gerri, and to experience some memorable barbecue, because Stephen is making noises about leaving the business soon to "go fishin'."

From U.S. 70 in Goldsboro, take U.S. 117 south 3.4 miles toward Mt. Olive. Turn left onto N.C. 581 South and go 4 miles, crossing the Neuse River. Turn right on to Arrington Bridge Road and go 3.5 miles to its intersection with Sleepy Creek Road. Grady's is on the right, in the fork of the two roads.

DILLARD'S BAR-B-Q
3921 Fayetteville Street
Durham, N.C. 27707
919-544-1587
Lunch and dinner Tuesday through Saturday

Dillard's is a minority-owned place on Durham's south side, where blacks and whites alike gather to eat the Bull City's best barbecue and soul food. The late Sam Dillard, a Mississippi native, founded the restaurant in 1952. Although he died in 1997, his family continues to operate the place much as it always has. Because Dillard was a very devout man, the sign outside still reminds satiated diners who take the trouble to look up Deuteronomy 8:3 that, as good as the food is at Dillard's, "man does not live by bread alone."

Food is served cafeteria style. Once customers fill their trays, they move to comfortable booths in a dining room decorated with pennants from ACC schools and the state's historically black colleges and universities.

The experience of getting through the serving line can range from an exercise in self-restraint to an episode of caution-to-the-winds recklessness. Succulent, juicy fried and barbecued chicken take their places beside tender, meaty pork ribs; tangy chopped barbecue; falling-apart pork chops in gravy; slow-cooked country-style steak; fresh, crispy fried fish; and, at the end of the week, pork chitterlings

Serving at Dillard's Bar-B-Q in Durham is cafeteria style.

or "chitlins." The seasonal vegetables include all kinds of snap beans and peas, collard greens, country-style cabbage, squash and onions, fried okra, fresh corn, sweet potatoes, macaroni and cheese, fried apples and much more, depending on the time of year.

It's been my observation that barbecue customs among North Carolina's African-Americans often cross or ignore the established boundaries between eastern- and Piedmont-style barbecue. For example, Dillard's serves barbecue that's very nicely seasoned and heavily moistened with a sauce containing not only vinegar and red pepper, but also tomato paste and mustard. This is not characteristic of either eastern- or Lexington-style sauce, but rather of South Carolina sauces. The pork is cooked in electric pits, rather than over wood coals, but that delicious signature sauce somehow manages to make up for this shortcoming. A serving or two of Dillard's savory and rather *wet* barbecue can lead to some serious addiction. I've enjoyed it many times during the past ten years, and somehow, it keeps drawing me back. By the way, Dillard's sauce is sold in Durham-area grocery stores, where it's very popular for use on both pork and chicken.

At Dillard's, a barbecue dinner comes with two vegetables. I usually choose macaroni and cheese and cabbage. The macaroni is crusty on top, yet creamy in the middle, with some real spiciness to it. The cabbage is well seasoned, slightly sweet, and still a bit firm, rather than overcooked. Crispy, light hush puppies, which are not overly sweet, and *very* sweet iced tea round out a memorable meal.

For years, Dillard's was well known for selling pork ribs at the old Durham Bulls' ballpark. They were advertised as "a buck a bone." While the Bulls' new stadium has a concession selling Dillard's chopped barbecue, the ribs are now offered only through catered events or at the restaurant. At the restaurant, they're still priced at a buck each.

To get to Dillard's from Interstate 85, take Exit 172 on to the Durham Freeway (N.C. 147), heading south. Take Exit 11 (N.C. 55/Alston Avenue) off the freeway and turn right on to South Alston Avenue. Stay straight until you reach Riddle Road. Turn right on to Riddle Road until you reach Fayetteville Street. Turn right on to Fayetteville Street. The restaurant is on the right.

BULLOCK'S BAR B CUE

✓ MAY '05 (?)

3330 Quebec Street
Durham, N.C. 27705
919-383-3211
Lunch and dinner Tuesday through Saturday

It's a tribute to the power of the word *barbecue* that an owner will often use the term in his restaurant's name, even if barbecue is only one among sixty or seventy items he serves. I knew one man who ran a place called Jack's Barbecue that didn't serve barbecue at all.

Since owner Tommy Bullock has specialized for years in catering pig pickin's, the term is certainly appropriate for his restaurant. However, Bullock's is really more of an emporium of all types of southern comfort food than it is a barbecue joint. The restaurant's varied, down-home menu is obviously on target because there's usually a big crowd waiting for the place to open for lunch. In fact, Bullock's has enjoyed heavy patronage practically since it first opened in 1952.

Bullock's has two large dining rooms, plus a glassed-in porch. I have never been to Bullock's when all three rooms weren't pretty well packed. Despite the constant hubbub in the place, a veteran waitress will quickly bring your drink, take your order, run through the daily specials, explain various choices, and take your order with the businesslike voice of a blackjack dealer.

Beginning with North Carolina pork barbecue and barbecued chicken and beef, the menu is extensive. It covers the whole range of country cooking: greens and vegetables of every description; chicken pie; country-style steak; ham; meat loaf; beef tips...you name it. You can also order lasagna; roast beef; a number of fried and broiled seafood choices; sandwiches of all types; salads; and more desserts than any of us need to consider.

Bullock's serves typical eastern-style barbecue, which is very finely chopped. Because it isn't pit-cooked, there is no smoky taste. The barbecue is purposely served a little on the bland side so customers can add the fiery vinegar-and-red-pepper sauce to satisfy their own tastes. Many will end up adding salt as well. Sweet, white coleslaw and moderately sweet, onion-flavored hush puppies accompany the barbecue. You can have these same side dishes when you order a plate dinner of crisp, tasty fried chicken or Brunswick stew.

Among the most popular desserts at Bullock's are homemade coconut and chocolate pie. The chocolate pie has a decadently rich, smooth filling; a flaky bottom crust; and a gorgeously browned, crisp meringue. The pie alone is worth a visit.

After many visits, I find that overall the barbecue and other dishes at Bullock's are of a consistently high quality. If very little is truly memorable, with the exception of that chocolate pie, I'm always pretty sure that nothing will fall very far short of the mark, either. Although the locals consistently give Bullock's an average score of around 75 points out of a possible 100, you have to remember that practically every time the doors swing open at 11:30 A.M., there's a crowd waiting to get in.

BARBEQUE HUT
3608 Ramsey Street (U.S. 401 Business)
Fayetteville, N.C. 28311
910-488-5674
All locations: Lunch and dinner Monday through Saturday

Other locations:
2802 Fort Bragg Road
910-485-5390

2965 Owen Drive
910-484-1975

It was "Old Hickory," President Andrew Jackson, who is supposed to have said, "It's a damned poor man who only knows one way to spell a word." According to that sentiment, you've got to love the folks at Barbeque Hut, who have three locations in Fayetteville. Not that it matters one whit to anyone, or that a single soul even notices,

Barbecue restaurants in the Piedmont (and some places in the east) cook pork shoulders rather than whole hogs.
DAN ROUTH PHOTOGRAPHY

but the sign in front of the location on Ramsey Street reads *Barbeque Hut.* Letters affixed to the building spell out *Barbecue Hut,* and a plaque recognizing the restaurant as the recipient of the *Fayetteville Observer*'s "Best Place for Barbecue" award for the year 2000 calls it *Bar-B-Que Hut.* That leaves the spellings *BBQ, Bar-B-Q, B-B-Cue,* and *B-B-Que* still to be used in some fashion around the place, and I'm confident the owners will get to all of them in time.

While we're on the subject of minor details, the logo for this place features an *angry*-looking pig wearing a chef's hat and holding a barbecue fork. This makes a lot of sense to me. I've always wondered why pigs are pictured looking happy on so many other barbecue restaurant signs. Would *you* look happy?

At this tiny little place, which truly resembles a hut, orders are placed at the counter. The building is neat on the outside, clean and attractive inside, and the friendly service and free iced-tea refills obviously make it popular with local residents.

I had a barbecue sandwich piled with chunky chopped pork. The pork was well moistened, with a sweet, vinegar-based sauce. The meat isn't pit-cooked, but it's *well* cooked, meaning moist and tender, and the seasoning is just right.

In addition to barbecue, Barbeque Hut, or however you decide to refer to it, has sandwiches and daily lunch specials. The day I was there, several customers were enjoying eye-catching plates of whole fried croakers, tails and all. They all looked like they'd been there many times before (the customers, not the fish). I believe you'll get a kick out of this place, and I look forward to going back.

CAPE FEAR BARBECUE
523 Grove Street
Fayetteville, N.C. 28301
910-483-1884
Lunch and dinner daily

This popular minority-owned place used to be a Smithfield's location, but it changed hands in 1999. The menu is similar to that of the eastern North Carolina chain, and the food is generally tasty and plentiful.

The restaurant is decorated with banners, athletic jerseys, and other memorabilia from Cape Fear High School, and the presence of a plaque expressing appreciation from the school's PTSA indicates some kind of special relationship between the owners and the high school. Having followed (and helped to finance) the activities of three children as they moved through secondary school, I like to see

Many barbecue lovers prefer meat that's been hand-chopped with a cleaver.
DAN ROUTH PHOTOGRAPHY

this kind of spirit and support, so I personally would go out of my way to patronize such a community-minded place.

Barbecue and fried chicken are the mainstays of the menu here. My barbecue sandwich was piled high with a generous serving of pork, which tasted very spicy and fresh and looked hand-chopped, but wasn't wood-cooked. The Brunswick stew was very acceptable, containing meaty chunks of pork, but I found it a little on the watery side and wondered about the inclusion of green beans, which—excuse me—just *don't* belong in Brunswick stew! The fried chicken, I'm happy to report, was right on target: crispy on the outside; tender, juicy, and well seasoned on the inside.

Cape Fear Barbecue is obviously run by enthusiastic, hard-working people who realize that life is about more than just business, and I think you'll have a pleasant barbecue experience here.

McCall's Barbecue and Seafood
139 Miller's Chapel Road (U.S.70 and N.C. 111)
Goldsboro, N.C. 27535
919-751-0072

A franchise location:
4251 Arendell Street (U.S. 70)
Morehead City, N.C. 28557
252-727-0600

Both locations: Lunch and dinner daily

Some people mistakenly characterize McCall's Barbecue and Seafood as a fish house that also happens to have barbecue, particularly if they've only sampled the chopped pork they find on the buffet. Actually, Randy McCall and Worth Westbrook turn out pit-cooked barbecue that's tender, smoky, and appetizing enough to be among the best in the east. But be advised: you should *always* order barbecue at McCall's directly from the menu. Frankly, barbecue just does not "hold" well in a steam table, and the freshly chopped and seasoned 'cue that's brought from the kitchen directly to your table is *much* superior to what many people might sample more or less in passing.

McCall and Westbrook start their whole-hog barbecue on their innovative Old Hickory pit. Loaded with racks of pig quarters, a Ferris wheel-like machine rotates inside a wood-and-charcoal-fired smoke chamber for eleven hours. After that, the meat is cooked on conventional, wood-burning pits for another several hours. Barbecued chicken is prepared the same way, although the cooking times are different. The result is meltingly tender barbecue with a delicious smoky taste, plus the extra flavor, which results when fat is allowed to drip directly onto wood coals beneath the cooking meat. The barbecue isn't seasoned according to predetermined measurements, but rather to taste, since the owners point out that "every pig is different."

McCall's barbecued chicken (order it directly off the menu, too) is tender, juicy, golden-brown, and flavorful. It has just enough charring of the crispy skin to add to the visual appeal.

Aside from McCall's barbecued foods, which also include ribs and pork skins, the popular lunch and dinner buffets have tasty country-style pork chops, fried chicken, seafood, a salad bar, a varying selection of vegetables, and several desserts. The menu contains a full selection of seafood and sandwiches in addition to barbecue, chicken, and rib plates.

A franchise McCall's location in Morehead City, which is not owned by McCall and Westbrook, cooks barbecue in the same way as the Goldsboro restaurant.

WILBER'S BARBECUE
4172 U.S. 70 East
Goldsboro, N.C. 27534
919-778-5218
Breakfast, lunch, and dinner daily

Opened in 1962, Wilber Shirley's landmark restaurant is now one of only a handful of restaurants in eastern North Carolina to still cook barbecue entirely over hardwood coals. Well-situated on busy U.S. 70, Wilber's Barbecue is routinely jammed by locals, regular travelers, and, during the summer, hundreds of thousands of beach goers.

As the plaques and framed write-ups hanging in the lobby attest, this is one of the most famous barbecue places in the United States. The reputation here wasn't built on the friendly, fast service inside the comfortable, pine-paneled dining rooms. Instead, it was built out behind the restaurant, where a long, low pit house and an enormous pile of stacked, split hardwood bear testimony to Shirley's insistence to sticking with the old-fashioned ways of cooking barbecue. Wilber has a crew cutting and splitting wood year-round. There's even someone who stays up all night—every night—burning the hardwood down to coals on an outside grate, then carrying the coals one shovelful at a time into the pit house where the coals are spread beneath the slow-roasting meat.

Wilber's barbecue is hand-chopped to an appetizing chunky texture. It isn't as dry as most eastern 'cue, which has a high proportion of white meat from the hams and loins. That's because Shirley cooks not only whole hogs, but also pork shoulders, which provide extra amounts of moist dark meat and additional shreds of the smoky, chewy "outside brown" that add visual appeal and rich flavor. The meat is served seasoned with salt and ground pepper, but otherwise unadorned with vinegar. Most people will want to add liberal amounts of Wilber's trademark sauce, which is one of the more complex and tasty eastern sauces I've encountered.

Wilber's has pit-cooked barbecued chicken, out-of-this-world fried chicken, ribs, all sorts of other country-style meats and vegetables, sandwiches, and tasty traditional desserts. There's even a complete breakfast menu. The main thing you'll remember, though, is the barbecue, which is some of the best you'll ever eat.

M&K BARBECUE & COUNTRY COOKIN'
U.S. 52
Granite Quarry, N.C. 28072
704-279-8976
Breakfast, lunch, and dinner Monday through Friday
Breakfast and lunch Saturday

The "M&K" comes from Moran and Kathy Thomas, who have seen their Granite Quarry restaurant prosper during the past several years. Occupying what was formerly a service station and garage, the restaurant used to have a large overhang or portico out front, with the dining room occupying what once was the waiting room. The barbecue was cooked out back in the former garage bay. Now the former portico area has been enclosed, doubling the dining space, and the owners have built an entirely new, modern pit house designed so the pork shoulders don't have to be turned during the ten or more hours it takes to cook them. One thing that hasn't changed, though, is the practice of cooking the barbecue over oak and hickory slabs. Moran Thomas claims that his is the last place in Rowan County that cooks barbecue entirely over wood, with no back-up help from electric or gas pits.

Thomas says he learned the art of barbecue from his father, who was passing along secrets learned from *his* father. Moran's grandfather reportedly sold open-pit barbecue off rough board tables to railroad workers and passengers in the town of Spencer during the early 1900s, perhaps even before legends-to-be Jess Swicegood and Sid Weaver set up their famed barbecue stands in Lexington. After driving a truck for a number of years, Moran Thomas returned to his roots, establishing M&K Barbecue & Country Cookin'. Here he continued to pit-cook the lean, tender, smoke-flavored barbecue that had been an important part of his family's history for nearly a century.

As to the "Country Cookin' " side of the business, M&K has plenty to offer: country-style steak, hamburger steak, stew beef, country ham, pork chops, and tempting vegetable selections such as okra, squash, pintos, cabbage, and macaroni and cheese.

This is also a fabulous place to get a good, messy, old-fashioned hamburger or cheeseburger—the kind that's practically guaranteed to leave grease stains on the front of your shirt. The cooks at M&K hand pat their own hamburgers and sausage, rather than using frozen patties. Thomas says he goes through 500 to 600 pounds of top-grade hamburger each week. Even though I didn't have an opportunity to try a burger at M&K, someone is obviously doing something right if those numbers are any indication. However, I can personally attest that the Lexington-style barbecue and fixin's that you get at M&K earn a letter grade of "A."

COUNTRY BAR-B-QUE
4012 Wendover Avenue
Greensboro, N.C. 27407
336-292-3557
Breakfast, lunch, and dinner Monday through Saturday

A cardiologist recommended this place to me, pronouncing it "the best barbecue in Greensboro." Praise for a barbecue joint coming from a cardiologist is pretty unusual. Now, I'm not going as far as proclaiming it the best barbecue place in Greensboro, since I'm still a big fan of Stamey's authentic wood-cooked barbecue across town. However, I will say that Country Bar-B-Que manages to keep its chopped barbecue chunky and moist, whereas some people feel the pork at Stamey's is chopped too finely and is thus a bit too dry.

Seeing no sign of a real pit or a woodpile around Country Bar-B-Que's plain brick building, I can only deduce that the barbecue here is cooked on electric or gas-fired pits. Although the meat is not noticeably smoky-tasting, it's tender, moist, and well seasoned. It is also served with an excellent Lexington-style dip. In addition, I tried the barbecued chicken, which is prepared on Tuesday, Thursday, and Saturday. I found it to be tender and flavorful without being overcooked, as this dish often can be.

The typical Lexington-style barbecue slaw is tasty and well seasoned. However, the hush puppies are the frozen variety, which is an unfortunate concession to convenience. Fortunately, they have recently added baked biscuits to the menu. You can also order hamburgers and hot dogs.

For dessert, I tried the homemade peach cobbler. Although I certainly thought it was very good, a very cute and precocious toddler in the booth next to mine rated it even more highly, exclaiming several times, "it's just the *best* peach cobbler I've ever tasted!"

Country Bar-B-Que opens for breakfast at 6:00 A.M. For those who don't want to leave their car, there's even a drive-up window for takeout orders.

To reach Country Bar-B-Que from Interstate 40, turn north on Wendover Avenue and look for the restaurant on the left.

Stamey's Old Fashioned Barbecue in Greensboro is one of North Carolina's most noted barbecue restaurants.

STAMEY'S OLD FASHIONED BARBECUE

2206 High Point Road
Greensboro, N.C. 27403
336-299-9888

Second location:
2812 Battleground Avenue
Greensboro, N.C. 27408
336-288-9275

Both locations: Lunch and dinner Monday through Saturday

C. Warner Stamey is the man more responsible than any other for spreading the fame of Lexington-style barbecue. After spending years perfecting the art of barbecuing in Lexington and Shelby, Warner opened the original Stamey's in Greensboro in 1953.

The latest structure to occupy the site, built in the 1980s, is probably North Carolina's most elaborate barbecue restaurant. The restaurant's prime location across High Point Road from the Greensboro Coliseum has contributed to generations of basketball fans spreading the word and making it one of North Carolina's best-known barbecue places.

But the reputation of Stamey's wasn't built on attractive surroundings or location. It was built on the fact that the place still cooks pork shoulders the same way Warner Stamey did it, beginning in the 1930s: over real hardwood coals. The restaurant's founder was constantly trying to design better pits, and Stamey's has a freestanding pit building that's far larger and more elaborate than any other in North Carolina. It has arched, brick fireplaces and totally enclosed brick pits. Customers are used to seeing a large pile of hardwood scraps piled in a corner of the parking lot, and they've come to expect that the barbecue they enjoy inside the restaurant will have an unmistakable wood-smoked flavor.

Stamey's offers its barbecue chopped or pulled, which they call "sliced." The restaurant does a tremendous volume, particularly at its drive-through, so it doesn't have time to hand-chop the barbecue. To my taste, the machine that shreds the meat gets it a little too fine. That's a minor point, however, and the barbecue is otherwise unfailingly moist, tender, and flavorful. The sauce is sweeter than most Lexington-style dips and is relatively mild, but Stamey's makes the most peppery barbecue slaw in North Carolina. The slaw is definitely the spiciest part of a Stamey's barbecue sandwich and complements the mildly flavored pork in the same way horseradish complements roast beef. The restaurant serves tiny, crescent-shaped hush puppies, which have a touch of sweetness. Most customers can't keep their fingers from reaching for "just one more."

Peach cobbler, which is best enjoyed with a scoop of vanilla ice cream, is the dessert of choice at Stamey's, outselling apple and cherry cobbler ten to one.

Chip Stamey, Warner's grandson, now runs this landmark restaurant, and the renowned barbecue pioneer would be proud to see that the family tradition is being so ably upheld.

B'S BARBECUE AND GRILL
N.C. 43 at B's Barbecue Road
Greenville, N.C. 27834
No telephone number
Lunch only Tuesday through Saturday

Housed in a former country store, B's Barbecue and Grill is one of eastern North Carolina's top spots for both pork barbecue and barbecued chicken.

In 1978, Bill and Peggy MacLawhorn established the restaurant as a way to get out of farming. Bill had been quite a well-known amateur pig cooker and thought he had a pretty good sauce recipe, so he and Peggy remodeled a former country store and built a screened pit house. Because of poor health Bill is no longer involved in running the business, but Peggy and her three daughters are usually on duty in the mini-cafeteria-style restaurant. A line of customers extends all the way out the screened front door and across the crowded gravel parking lot on most days. Around to the side, there's a second line for the takeout window. In pleasant weather, you can order from the takeout and eat at one of several picnic tables placed beneath the shade of a large tree.

The barbecue at B's comes from whole hogs cooked over hardwood charcoal. Well-smoked from the charcoal pit, the barbecue is only lightly seasoned, so you'll probably want to add a splash of B's spirited vinegar-and-pepper sauce. It's bottled in a random collection of recycled containers, including old Canadian Club whiskey bottles. Whole sets of tender, meaty ribs from the cooked hogs are available for around ten to twelve dollars a set. A set is enough to fill a large foil pan. Although they're devoid of any sticky-sweet sauce, they're extraordinary.

B's is as well known for its barbecued chicken as for its pork barbecue. Half chickens are slow-cooked over coals with no basting. After cooking for hours, the chickens are immersed for a short time in a vinegar-based sauce similar to the one used on the barbecue. Unlike a lot of barbecued chicken served in eastern North Carolina, B's version isn't overdone to the point where it's sliding off the bone. The crusty brown skin maintains a nice crispness, even after the half chicken is dunked in sauce. The complex, pit-cooked flavors are tantalizing beyond description. I don't believe it's an overstatement to say that this is the best barbecued chicken I've ever encountered.

Along with the pork barbecue and chicken, B's offers a scrumptious selection of home-style vegetables. They also serve delicious squares of baked corn bread as an interesting alternative to the usual hush puppies.

Since B's closes in the early afternoon, you'll want to visit at lunchtime. To get there if you're approaching Greenville from Wilson on U.S. 264, stay straight on U.S. 264 Business, rather than turning onto the U.S. 264 Bypass. At the first traffic light, turn left on B's Barbecue Road and go 1.2 miles to the intersection with N.C. 43. B's is on the right at the intersection.

PARKER'S BARBECUE
3109 South Memorial Drive
Greenville, N.C. 27828
252-756-2388
Lunch and dinner daily

Years ago, the Parker family divided up the family barbecue business. Former employees now run Parker's in Wilson, while Parker's kinfolks operate Parker's on busy South Memorial Drive (N.C. 11) in Greenville. The menus are similar at the two locations, but the restaurants are under totally different management and are not the same.

The Greenville Parker's is what I call a "filling station," offering safe, predictable food, and lots of it, to people who don't like to get too adventurous with their dining. The place specializes in barbecue dinners, which include the pork itself, Brunswick stew, coleslaw, boiled potatoes or French fries, and corn sticks. You can also get a barbecue plate, which includes only barbecue, slaw, and corn sticks. You can add fried chicken to the barbecue dinner and make it a "family-style dinner." Fried fish, shrimp, oysters, and even oyster stew are also available.

Parker's has become a household name in eastern North Carolina, not because the food is outstanding or even very noteworthy, but because people know what to expect every time they visit. As a result, the Greenville Parker's, like the one in Wilson, does a tremendous business.

Since wood-cooked flavor is not often even *expected* of barbecue in eastern North Carolina, the customers at the Greenville Parker's have no problem with the fact that the meat isn't pit-cooked and doesn't taste the least bit smoky. It has a strong vinegar flavor, particularly when you add a little of the house sauce. This sauce is peppery-hot without the slightest hint of sugar. The yellow eastern-style slaw also has a strong vinegar flavor, and to my taste, lacks other seasoning. Personally, I also found the Brunswick stew rather bland.

The boiled potatoes, served with a dash of paprika, admirably balance the tartness of the barbecue. Parker's also serves crunchy corn sticks, which are ten-inch bars of corn bread that are first baked, then deep fried. I thought the potatoes and corn sticks were the best dishes on the menu. The fried chicken is so-so—hot and filling but providing little excitement.

Let me hasten to say that Parker's has obviously found an important niche among thousands of eastern North Carolina diners and barbecue lovers. If I find the food somewhat generic, there are undoubtedly many others who think it's terrific. Parker's gets high marks for cleanliness and consistency, so if that's what important to you, you'll love the place.

J&G BAR-B-QUE
2703 North Church Street
Haw River, N.C. 27258
336-578-0729
Lunch and dinner Thursday through Saturday

J&G Bar-b-que is one of those places where the food seems generic at first, but then it grows on you. I have to say that although nothing stands out about the barbecue or other dishes, the overall impression is very good and the whole ends up being more than the sum of all its parts.

This place used to be known as "Jakes." It's located just outside the Burlington city limits in the community of Haw River. Even though J&G is close to the blue-collar east side of Burlington, it's still the favorite spot for barbecue among many of the aging residents of Burlington's more affluent west side. Many of these patrons adopted the modest establishment as something of a hangout when they were in high school during the 1960s, since it was located on the "cruising" route.

The barbecue here isn't pit-cooked over wood, but it's unusual enough to be interesting. The meat on the barbecue plates and trays that are brought to your table is covered with a brown, silty layer of vinegar and pepper that looks almost like a paste. Despite how it may sound, the barbecue is quite tasty, especially since it's tender, adequately salted, and not too finely chopped. This is almost eastern-style barbecue, with no tomato or sugar in evidence in the spicy seasoning, which is really not liquid enough to properly be called a sauce.

J&G is another of those barbecue joints where people bow neither toward the east nor toward Lexington. As a result, it suffers from coleslaw schizophrenia. Since the slaw contains mayonnaise *and* ketchup, the resulting shocking-pink concoction straddles the fence between the white slaw of the east and the red slaw found further west.

J&G may have the best hush puppies in North Carolina. Light and crispy, with enough flour in the batter to allow them to hold together and fry up golden brown, they are smooth-skinned, rather than crusty. Not overly burdened with sugar nor overpowered with onion, J&G's pups are fried at precisely the right temperature to prevent their soaking up too much of the frying oil.

If you need to find the rest room, be forewarned that it's outside. Well, it isn't literally outside, but since there's no connecting door, you have to go outside to get to it. Searching for the facilities is just another adventure in barbecue-land, and well worth the trouble in order to enjoy the 'cue and those great hush puppies.

NUNNERY-FREEMAN BARBECUE
Norlina Road (U.S. 158)
Henderson, N.C. 27536
252-438-4751
Lunch and dinner Tuesday through Sunday

Same ownership: Gary's Barbecue
140 Zeb Robinson Road (near Maria Parham Hospital)
Henderson, N.C. 27536
252-430-7144
Lunch and dinner Tuesday through Sunday

In a 1997 article, my friend and former fellow UNC cheerleader, Jack Betts of the *Charlotte Observer*, pronounced this outwardly nondescript establishment his favorite Tar Heel barbecue stop. Despite the fact that the meat isn't cooked over wood, I have to agree that it's top-drawer. The barbecue is prepared on a Kook-Rite Kooker™, a commercial electric pit built by Nunnery-Freeman Manufacturing in Henderson. The pork for this restaurant is actually cooked across town at Gary's Barbecue, a newer establishment under the same ownership

The flat-topped, 1960s-style tan brick building houses a big, square dining room with windows all around. Its booths and tables are generally full of loyal local customers. They're attracted by a menu that includes not only barbecue and its usual fixin's, but also

lots of home-style vegetables, fried chicken, se
selection of sandwiches.

The barbecue is extremely tasty and quite moist, des,
that it is obviously chopped by machine rather than by ha..
(Sometimes this causes chopped pork to dry out a bit.) Although
the sauce definitely falls into the broad category of eastern-style
and vinegar-based, it's a little sweeter than most. It is still full-
bodied, with a mature dose of ground red pepper. You can even buy
a bottle to take home.

Nunnery-Freeman Barbecue serves a very creditable Brunswick
stew, which contains the proper ingredients of chicken, pork,
tomatoes, corn, lima beans, onions, and spices. It does not have
potatoes, but they are optional in a true Brunswick stew. The
mixture lacks the hint of sweetness characteristic of other stews in
this part of North Carolina. I personally enjoyed my portion more
after I stirred in the contents of one of the sugar packets on the
table. Jack Betts opines that Nunnery-Freeman has the best stew in
the Piedmont. The only exception I would take to that opinion is to
question whether Henderson is truly part of the Piedmont. It may
be on the borderline geographically, but the atmosphere and
customs found in Henderson indicate that it should be considered
an eastern North Carolina community. In any case, the stew's good
and the sugar is free, so you can satisfy your own personal taste.

A very fine iced tea and small, light, crispy hush puppies with a
robust onion flavor set off my meal. The banana pudding looked
good, but the barbecue was just a little too good for me to save
room.

Nunnery-Freeman Barbecue is located near Exit 215 off
Interstate 85. Gary's Barbecue is near Exit 212.

KEPLEY'S BARBECUE

1304 North Main Street
High Point, N.C. 27262
336-884-1021
Lunch and dinner Monday through Saturday

Kepley's is still located in the corrugated-metal building perpendicular to High Point's North Main Street where it first opened for business in 1948. The paneled, L-shaped interior has seen a lot of customers come and go over the years, and Kepley's has attracted the long-time loyalty of most of them.

Just about everyone who talks about how good the barbecue is at Kepley's makes some reference to it being a big part of their growing-up experience in High Point, or they remark that it's been their very favorite barbecue since they were a child. Furthermore, it seems that at least half the customers who come in for takeout orders tell owner Bob Burleson (who, with his wife Susan, has been around for all but six years of the restaurant's existence) that they've been getting barbecue from Kepley's for their entire life. Burleson does a big business selling barbecue by the pound for entertaining at home, and he says he ships it to quite a few loyal former customers in distant locations.

All this just goes to show you the power of pleasant childhood associations, or it could be due to the genial, white-haired Burleson's kindly air, because by the area's standards (Lexington is just a few miles away, after all), Kepley's barbecue is actually rather unremarkable to my taste.

Not that there's a thing wrong with it, mind you, but despite being called "pit-cooked barbecue," it tastes as though it's cooked on an electric or gas cooker, with nothing very memorable added in the way of seasoning. Actually, the overall taste of the barbecue and sauce is very vinegary, compared to Lexington's sweeter aftertaste. In fact, Kepley's chopped pork could almost be labeled an eastern-style barbecue, except that it's prepared from shoulders and hams, rather than the whole hog. The slaw, too, is vinegar-based and not as sweet as some versions, while the hush puppies are cooked to a deep brown, with a grainy texture on the outside. You'll have a pleasant barbecue meal at Kepley's, but not, to my thinking, a mountaintop experience.

Well, you certainly can't argue with success, and Kepley's has earned plenty of that over the years. I'm sure Bob and Susan Burleson are proud of their legion of loyal fans, and there's a lesson here about the importance of a pleasant atmosphere in shaping customers' perceptions about the food itself.

CLARK'S BAR-B-Q
1331 N.C. 66 South
Kernersville, N.C. 27284
336-996-8989 or 996-8644
Lunch and dinner daily

The town of Kernersville, located off Interstate 40 Business between Greensboro and Winston-Salem, is best known for being a fast-growing bedroom community and for Körner's Folly, an odd, 22-room structure built in the late 1800s by decorator/designer/painter Jule Körner. Körner was famous for painting Bull Durham Tobacco bulls on buildings across the Southeast. Inside the "Folly," eccentric nooks and crannies, trap doors, and child-sized rooms alternate with or open into elegant, high-ceilinged spaces. It's said that no two doorways are exactly alike.

We're happy to report that nearby Clark's Bar-B-Q will transport you from the fanciful to the no-nonsense. This is even evident from its location in an unprepossessing, rectangular brick building on N.C. 66 south of Kernersville, between the business and bypass sections of Interstate 40. The interior decoration and ambiance are equally unremarkable, but the owner of Clark's certainly resembles the imaginative young Körner in that no two spellings of the word "barbecue" are alike on the restaurant's premises. It's spelled *Bar-B-Q* in the sign atop the building, *Barebeque* on the sign behind the counter, *Barbecue* on the menu, and *BBQ* on the label of Clark's own brand of sauce. Four different spellings at a single barbecue joint represent a North Carolina record!

But you get a deep, solid feeling about Clark's when you make the obligatory swing around the building before parking and see a neatly stacked woodpile. This feeling is reinforced during mid-afternoon when wisps of smoke still drift from the smokestacks of the brick pit's chimneys. Although the pork shoulders go on the pits before dawn, they don't reach a perfect state of doneness until around 6:00 P.M.

My barbecue sandwich was good, solid, middle-of-the-road Lexington-style fare. The meat was lean and chopped to the right consistency; the smoke flavor from the wood-burning pits was suitably in evidence; and the Lexington dip and barbecue slaw were pretty much textbook offerings. One unusual touch is that Clark's serves circular-shaped hush puppies that resemble fat onion rings.

This place gets good reviews from patrons of some of the barbecue chat rooms, from traveling salesmen, and from employees of the giant Roadway Express truck terminal next door. What more could you ask for?

Clark's is located on N.C. 66 South, between Interstate 40 and Interstate 40 Business.

Prissy Polly's

729 N.C. 66 South
Kernersville, N.C. 27284
336-993-5045
Lunch and dinner Monday through Saturday

Okay, I know what you're probably wondering, so let's get it out of the way right up front. This place got its name from the nickname pinned on owner Loren Whaley's mother. Whaley must have figured that someone named Prissy Polly would fit right into the fabric of life in Kernersville, home of the annual Honey Bee Festival and something called the Spring Folly.

Whaley is originally from eastern North Carolina. When he opened Prissy Polly's in 1991, the idea was to create a niche by serving strictly eastern-style North Carolina barbecue in the heathen territory of the Piedmont. Whaley studied the preparation of eastern North Carolina barbecue under the tutelage of easterner Doug Saul, who has operated barbecue places in several towns over the years. Whaley obviously made a course correction along the way, because nowadays his place serves both an authentic eastern-style barbecue and what an easterner might imagine Lexington-style might taste like if they had never eaten any. Don't get me wrong—that *other* barbecue served by Prissy Polly's is tasty. I'd happily eat it again, but I'm not quite sure it's really Lexington-style barbecue. (Oh, *stop it*. This is barbecue, not brain surgery, and Whaley serves up some good pig, whatever it's called.)

Prissy Polly's is a tiny place that serves cafeteria style, with the serving line on one side and the dining room on the other. Although I was initially disappointed not to see a woodpile or evidence of a real, smoke barbecue pit, I immediately liked the inside's genteel untidiness. It is right in line with some of the best barbecue places I've encountered. The radio broadcasting the Wake Forest basketball game and the Demon Deacon basketball poster on the wall tipped me off right away to the fact that Whaley is probably a Wake supporter. The framed religious slogans let me know that he, or someone, is serious about his faith.

I ordered a combination plate, with a little of each style of barbecue, an order of Brunswick stew, and one interesting-looking pork sparerib. I then sat at one of the compact dining room's square, highly varnished tables with short picnic benches on each side.

As I had expected, the eastern-style barbecue was pretty much right on target, and I appreciated the fact that it wasn't too finely chopped. The "Lexington-style" barbecue was tasty, tender, and well moistened with a sauce that was a little too thick and contained a little too much tomato sauce to win authentic Lexington credentials. But as I say, it was good nonetheless. The meat's long, string-like fibers indicate it may have come from the rib area of a pig, rather than the shoulder, which is the traditional Lexington cut. Neither version of barbecue had any evidence of smoke flavor. No surprise there, since I saw no evidence of wood cooking when I first came in.

The Brunswick stew, offered on the cafeteria line as a vegetable choice, was fairly authentic, with plenty of onions and pepper. The pork rib was glazed with a mild sauce and attractively dotted with grains of coarse black pepper. The rib meat was a *slight* bit on the firm side, but still very enjoyable. I personally prefer ribs with the meat falling right off the bone.

Prissy Polly's is definitely worth a stop when you're nearby. As an additional bonus, you'll get a kick out of answering if someone asks you where you ate lunch or dinner.

Prissy Polly's is located on N.C. 66 South, between Interstate 40 and Interstate 40 Business.

Stratford BBQ II

King-Tobaccoville Road
King, N.C. 27021
336-983-0263
Lunch and dinner Monday through Saturday

Stratford BBQ II (I'm not sure where BBQ I is or was) makes much of the fact that the barbecue here is cooked with hickory wood, and the area behind the restaurant does indeed boast a big pile of hickory slabs.

However, I should point out that there are four key factors in preparing great barbecue: tenderness, consistency, wood-smoked flavor, and seasoning. Since the smoked flavor can only carry you so far (and since some people don't like it anyway), it's important to make sure the meat is always cooked long enough and at a low-enough temperature for the barbecue to stay moist and for the meat fibers to relax into that perfect state of tenderness. Many pit masters wrap the shoulders in foil for the last two or three hours on the pit, which works wonders, tenderizing the meat and holding in moisture. After the meat is cooked, it's important to pull it from the bones and to add enough seasoning so that it has some flavor aside from the sauce.

At Stratford II, I found the barbecue flavorful but a little dry, at least on the particular day I visited. It could very well be that my experience was an anomaly and that I happened to be served meat from a single shoulder that had gotten a bit dried out, which can easily happen anywhere. If a restaurant's management is willing to go to the trouble to cook with wood, I'll certainly cut them some slack for having a less than perfect day, so I'm sure I'll be making another visit to Stratford.

There is a complete selection of sandwiches, and there are plate lunches and dinners (including some seafood), but aside from the pit-cooked barbecue, the place's biggest claims to fame are probably the hot dog and the foot-long hot dog. There are also some really good homemade cakes, including chocolate cake and pound cake. I also saw people enjoying some mighty good-looking peach and cherry cobbler.

J&L'S BARBECUE
1600 North Queen Street
Kinston, N.C. 28501
252-523-1005
Lunch and dinner daily; until 5:00 P.M. on Sunday

When most people think of barbecue in Kinston, they tend to think of present and former establishments on U.S. 70, Kinston's most heavily beaten track. However, J&L's Barbecue, located right in front of the big K-Mart on the north side of town, is a pleasant discovery. It's particularly welcome because it's one of the few barbecue restaurants open on Sunday. I'm personally not that fond of *any* place that opens on Sunday, but as long as people regard eating out as part of their day of rest, someone is going to have to fix the food. It might as well be barbecue as anything else.

Owner Earl Garner (no relation that I'm aware of) opened this restaurant in 1990. The tan and brick-red building with gold trim that houses J&L's appears to be a former fast-food place. Before owning his own place, Garner built his barbecue resumé at the Barbecue Lodge and Wilber's, two barbecue institutions located on U.S. 70.

J&L's Barbecue is a small place, where customers order at the counter toward the back, then carry their orders to compact tables up front. Although I noticed that there was no woodpile outside, I decided to check out the barbecue anyway. I don't know whether Garner cooks in an electric or gas-fired pit, but I was pleasantly surprised to find that he serves very lean, clean, savory barbecue, which is seasoned to perfection. It's served fairly well moistened with a vinegar-based, fairly sweet sauce, and there's more sauce on the tables to add according to taste. I enjoyed excellent light hush puppies and top-notch coleslaw, which tasted fresh and was not overloaded with mayonnaise.

I noticed that J&L's advertises a barbecue sandwich served on corn bread, a local peculiarity I have seen nowhere else but in the Kinston vicinity.

The restaurant also specializes in baked, barbecued, and fried chicken. It also serves seafood every day. The seafood must be pretty decent, because I saw a lot of orders being served the day I stopped in. Hamburgers, steaks, and fried pork chops are also on the menu, along with a selection of vegetables.

KING'S BARBECUE & CHICKEN
405 East New Bern Road (U.S. 70)
Kinston, N.C. 28501
252-527-2101
Lunch and dinner Monday through Friday
Breakfast, lunch, and dinner Saturday and Sunday
Special buffet on Sunday; takeout available daily from 9:00 A.M. to 9:00 P.M.

King's Barbecue & Chicken has been a familiar landmark to millions of travelers journeying up and down U.S. 70. These travelers include beach vacationers, who sometimes combine a visit to King's with a stop at the nearby Neuse Sports Shoppe.

King's has been around since 1936, when Frank King Sr. owned a country store on the site. A poolroom in the back became the first restaurant when King started feeding the pool players by heating canned foods from the store on a pot-bellied stove. During the 1950s, the site was a teenage hangout, and the back parking lot was said to be the biggest lover's lane in the area.

Now, King's is one of the largest restaurants in the South, seating 800 and serving an average of 8,000 pounds of barbecue, 6,000 pounds of chicken, and 1,500 pounds of collard greens each month. I find it amusing that King's sign is mounted on the same tall poles as the sign for the adjacent Piggly-Wiggly supermarket. The Piggly-Wiggly "smiling pig" logo in the middle of the pole appears to serve double duty for both the barbecue restaurant and the grocery store.

King's has several large, clean, attractive rooms, which are opened or closed according to traffic at any particular time. The dining room used most often has red-checked tablecloths on the booths around the walls and the tables in the room's central area.

I found that my plate of pork barbecue glistened with a delicious, typical eastern North Carolina vinegar-and-pepper sauce. I had especially crisp, tasty French fries, which were even better after being sprinkled with some of the same sauce. The barbecued chicken on my combination plate had a fairly thick, red sauce, unusual in this part of the state, where thin vinegar mixtures are the norm. For dessert, I tried a serving of King's appetizing banana pudding, topped with meringue, in an edible waffle bowl. I also noticed that there was a nice-looking array of pies available.

King's also features barbecued turkey, beef brisket, and pork ribs. There are down-home favorites, such as hamburger steak, country ham, and pork chops; seafood platters; and even grilled steak. The many daily specials include such dishes as chicken pastry, meat loaf, stew beef, and roast chicken. These dishes are supplemented with a wide variety of seasonal vegetable choices. Finally, there's a large sandwich menu, including the "pig in a puppy," which is pork barbecue piled on an especially large hush puppy.

Overall, King's serves very high-quality food of every type and does a wonderful job of merchandising everything from its barbecue sauce and other packaged items to its "Oink Express" barbecue shipping service. By calling 1-800-322-OINK, you can send dry-ice-packaged barbecue and fixin's to just about anywhere.

KNIGHTDALE SEAFOOD & BARBECUE
706 Money Court
Knightdale, N.C. 27545
919-266-4447
Lunch and dinner daily

Knightdale Seafood & Barbecue occupies a relatively new

building just off U.S. 64, not far from its old location. Aside from the conventional exterior appearance and the restaurant's rather ordinary name, the place absolutely defies characterization.

On the one hand, Knightdale Seafood & Barbecue serves absolutely traditional (though non-pit-cooked) eastern-style barbecue, and it actually won *Spectator* magazine's "Best Barbecue in the Triangle" award for the year 2000. To go with the well-seasoned barbecue, there are terrific light, crisp hush puppies, which were also recognized in several readers' picks, conventional-recipe Brunswick stew, and incredibly sweet tea—an eastern North Carolina icon if there ever was one.

The fried chicken, also a traditional favorite, is excellent. It looks and tastes as though it's been cooked in a pan rather than a deep fryer.

On the other hand, continuing a trend that began even before the location change, the restaurant also offers an eclectic, non-traditional menu, featuring a few attention-grabbing entrées like buffalo stew and ostrich steak. There's fried seafood, as you would expect, but the menu also includes crab legs and both tuna and salmon, available either blackened or grilled. The restaurant serves country-style pork chops with gravy from time to time, but it also offers prime rib and a selection of Certified Angus Beef steaks.

Perhaps because of the variety on the menu, one poll of Triangle area residents awarded Knightdale Seafood & Barbecue the designation of the area's "Best Place to Have Dinner." The barbecue, chicken, and fried seafood are all good, the other more upscale selections seem to get high marks from customers, and the place just seems to have an enjoyable atmosphere of mild adventure.

Barbecue is served Wednesday and Saturday only at B.J.'s Grill and BBQ in LaGrange.

B.J.'S GRILL AND BBQ

7823 U.S. 70 East
LaGrange, N.C. 28551
252-566-4702
Breakfast and lunch until 2:00 P.M. Monday through Saturday; dinner from 4:00 to 8:00 P.M. on Friday
Barbecue is served on Wednesday and Saturday only!

If you can't find what you're hungry for at B.J.'s Grill and BBQ, you may be just too darn hard to please. This neat-as-a-pin spot beside U.S. 70 has a menu that's absolutely covered with fine print. Breakfast, which is served from 4:00 A.M. on, takes up one-third of a tri-fold sheet. Daily lunch specials, barbecue, the Friday night dinner menu, and sandwiches take up the other two-thirds. The children's menu and desserts are on the back.

Although B.J.'s didn't open until 1980, by 1986 it had already won the contest for "Best Barbecue Down East," sponsored by the area's NBC affiliate, WITN-TV. The whole-hog pork is extremely lean and, unlike some finely chopped eastern North Carolina barbecue, is hand-chopped to a fairly coarse consistency. In my opinion, B.J's style helps retain the meat's moisture and tenderness.

B.J.'s serves its barbecue with a wonderful mild, sweet sauce that's equally popular around the restaurant as a dressing for steak, collard greens, pizza, and other foods. Referring to the sauce, owner B.J. Thigpen, a hard-working, no-nonsense woman, says confidently, "That'll be my retirement." Her husband Darrell, who helps run the place, introduced me to an interesting twist on barbecue. He served me a small plate of barbecue, moistened with sauce and mingled with chopped, raw onion. He had already discovered what I found—that these tastes somehow balance perfectly, producing an absolutely delicious combination. I'm not sure yet whether this is true of other barbecue or just B.J.'s, but I'm conducting further research.

On Thursday, B.J.'s barbecues chickens and whole 30- to 40-pound turkeys. The chickens and turkeys are seasoned with the same sweet, vinegar-based sauce and chopped just like the pork barbecue.

For dessert, be sure to try one of the homemade applejacks made with dried apples.

Remember, if you're looking for pork barbecue, you'll have to plan to be at B.J.'s on either Wednesday or Saturday, since these are the only days of the week that it's served.

Ken's Grill

7645 U.S. 70 West
LaGrange, N.C. 28551
252-566-4765
Breakfast, lunch, and dinner Monday through Saturday
Barbecue is served on Wednesday and Saturday only!

Located on U.S. 70 between Goldsboro and Kinston, Ken's Grill has become one of my favorite stopping places in eastern North Carolina. In part, this is because of the warm welcome I always get from Ken and David Eason, but it's also because of several dishes that this place prepares as well as anyone on the planet, including the barbecue, which is prepared on Wednesday and Saturday only.

David and Ken Eason of Ken's Grill in LaGrange

Ken's is one of the places that can really take the wind out of the sails of people like me who are always yapping about the importance of cooking barbecue over real wood coals. I had heard about Ken's barbecue by word of mouth long before I ever tried any first-hand. When I first tasted it myself, it was so terrific I just assumed it was pit-cooked. It was only after I had pronounced it some of the best I had ever eaten that I found out that it's cooked on an ordinary electric pit, and that the secret, at least in this case, must lie in the sauce and the seasonings.

Ken and David inherited their barbecue skills from their father, who operated Skin's Drive-In, located nearby. During the time he ran the drive-in, the elder Eason began cooking barbecue on Saturdays only. When he died in 1974, Ken took over the operation. When he built the present restaurant in 1980, Ken expanded the weekly barbecue days to include both Saturday and Wednesday.

Whatever it is that makes the barbecue so great must begin on that electric cooker, because the meat is, first of all firm, yet very, very tender. It's then seasoned so skillfully that a great many people, knowing full well that it isn't wood-cooked, have said it's the best they've ever had, and I'd be hard-pressed to argue with them. Chopped only to a coarse consistency; moistened with a fine, salty eastern blend of vinegar and pepper; then piled on a lightly steamed bun and topped with a crunchy white slaw, one of Ken's sandwiches leaves a wonderful, lingering aftertaste long after the sandwich is consumed.

Be sure to try one of his crispy pieces of pork skin, too.

Ken's also makes delicious hush puppies in a manner that I've never seen anywhere else. Piling the thick, cornmeal batter on top of a large, flat pancake turner, the cook trowels it flat, evens up the edges with a knife, then quickly cuts down through the batter, pushing half-inch "fingers" of batter off the end of the turner and into the frying oil.

If you're passing by Ken's on a day other than Wednesday or Saturday, I'd suggest one of his terrific, incredibly messy, hand-patted cheeseburgers (with chili). On Fridays in the winter, his tomato-based fish stew, containing poached eggs, has every one of the 70 seats in the place filled by local patrons. But, in truth, everything I've ever had at Ken's is good, and there's little chance you'll go wrong with any item on the menu.

Take a few minutes to get to know Ken and David (if they aren't too rushed), because they're both really nice guys who take a lot of pride in feeding people well.

BARBECUE CENTER

900 North Main Street
Lexington, N.C. 27292
336-248-4633
Breakfast, lunch, and dinner Monday through Saturday
Curb service offered

Barbecue Center is the most readily visible of Lexington's many barbecue restaurants for a couple of reasons. First, it's very close to U.S. 64, and it's the first barbecue place you'll see as you head into

Barbecue Center cooks over hardwood coals on North Main Street in downtown Lexington.
DAN ROUTH PHOTOGRAPHY

downtown Lexington from the north on U.S. 29/70. If you need a barbecue fix right away, it's the place to go. Secondly, the outdoor pits at Barbecue Center are usually where local, national, and international TV crews get footage of pork shoulders being cooked in advance of the annual Lexington Barbecue Festival.

Sonny Conrad's restaurant, in which his wife Nancy and two sons Michael and Cecil are all involved, is one of a declining number of Lexington barbecue restaurants where the pork shoulders are still cooked entirely over hardwood coals. Sonny's grandfathers on both sides of the family were adept at pit cooking, so he heard his call at an early age. He has now passed along the art and tradition of Lexington barbecue not only to his sons but also (albeit in less detail) to many curious customers who have taken home one of his written handouts on the subject. Pit-cooking instructions are also now posted on the Conrads' website at **www.barbecuecenter.com**.

Just a former drive-in where you can still get curb service or dine inside in fairly Spartan surroundings, Barbecue Center is nothing fancy. But, the barbecue here is a superb example of what Lexington barbecue is all about: moist and tender, with an appetizing texture, and a soft feel on the tongue. It's sprinkled with shreds of dark, smoky outside meat and is naturally mild and sweet, even before the addition of Lexington's trademark semi-sweet dip. The shoulders cook for nine hours or more, until the outside meat is dark and crusty, and the bones lift out easily without a shred of meat clinging to them.

Barbecue Center also features old-fashioned, hand-dipped banana splits. Since the desserts take about fifteen minutes each to make, the folks behind the counter have become a source of summer evening entertainment for customers and their children.

Cook's Barbecue serves wood-cooked barbecue at a secluded location off N.C. 8 near Lexington.
DAN ROUTH PHOTOGRAPHY

COOK'S BARBECUE
366 Valiant Drive
Lexington, N.C. 27292
336-798-1928
Lunch and dinner Wednesday through Sunday

All right, stick with me now, because this may get confusing. Doug Cook, who opened this rustic place off N.C. 8 in the Cotton Grove community during the late 1960s, doesn't own it any more, but it still bears his name. Cook now owns Backcountry Barbecue, another out-of-the-way place, which *doesn't* bear his name. Actually, Cook doesn't even live in North Carolina any more. He raises horses in Colorado, but he comes back to

Lexington to check on things from time to time.

Cook was one of the first to play around with the idea of operating a chain of barbecue restaurants, but apparently it never really worked out. He was also one of the first to experiment with electric cookers that had a chamber in which you could put green wood to smolder and produce smoke. Cook's Barbecue, which really isn't Cook's, used such an electric smoker at one time, but now it has gone back to cooking with real, honest-to-God hardwood in old-fashioned pits. Got all that?

Actually, all you really need to know is how to find this place (along with the fact that you *should* find it, because it serves really good barbecue). Getting there is a bit of an adventure (directions follow later). From the look of some of the signs you pass, you'll wonder whether the place went out of business years ago. However, when you pull into the parking area of what looks like a hunting camp in the woods, you'll begin having that thrill of anticipation that something good is getting ready to happen.

Inside the rough-wood-sided structure, there's a small front room, with unusual stainless steel-topped tables, picnic benches, distressed-wood paneling, and a fireplace. In the back, there's a larger, paneled room, also with a fireplace.

The presence of a salad bar indicates there are other offerings, but believe me, barbecue is the main deal here. Pork shoulders are pit-cooked 'til they're the shade of cordovan leather and falling-apart tender. The meat is then served chopped, coarse-chopped, or sliced, with a little cup of warm Lexington dip. Round hush puppies the size of cherry tomatoes and very finely chopped barbecue slaw both get good marks but are, frankly, almost beneath notice compared to the richly flavored, crusty meat. If you order sweet tea—and it's v-e-r-y sweet—they bring you a whole pitcher of it, which is a really nice touch.

Cook's is also the only barbecue restaurant in Lexington to serve pit-cooked beef brisket, in addition to pork shoulders. The brisket is smoky, tender, and very good, but it doesn't begin to compare to the pork, at least not in my book.

The restaurant also has barbecued chicken, hamburger steaks, fish, salads, and sandwiches. The homemade cobblers include cherry, peach, and strawberry.

But as I said, the barbecue is the main deal here.

To find Cook's Barbecue, head south on N.C. 8 through the Cotton Grove area, heading toward High Rock Lake. Turn right on Rockcrusher Road. Go ½ mile, then turn left on Valiant Drive. Go 0.2 mile to the end of the lane, where you'll see the unpainted wooden building on the right in a grove of trees.

JIMMY'S BBQ
1703 Cotton Grove Road (N.C. 8 South)
Lexington, N.C. 27292
336-357-2311
Breakfast, lunch, and dinner Wednesday through Monday

There are two things that really distinguish Jimmy Harvey's place. The first is his barbecued chicken. Prepared Thursday through Sunday, it is considered among the best in North Carolina. Thursday seems to be the biggest barbecued chicken day among the locals, so on that day, you'll probably have trouble getting to one of Jimmy's 125 seats without waiting awhile. Half chickens are cooked "low and slow" for hours, until they're deeply browned and the meat begins to slide off the bones. Then the chickens are brushed with sauce so that the crisp skin softens ever so slightly. Whether you prefer to enjoy the chicken as is or want to add more of Jimmy's peppery dip, which is among the hottest in town, you'll be in for an incredible treat.

The second unique characteristic is the fact that of all the family-run barbecue restaurants in North Carolina, this one may have the *most* family members employed. It's very difficult to keep up with them all, but at last report there were Jimmy; his wife Betty; two sons, Terry (the manager) and Kemp; and two daughters, Kirksey and Karen, working in the restaurant full-time, plus up to a half-dozen grandchildren who work when they're needed. This close-knit family even vacations together at High Rock Lake when they're off, and its members are representative of the sense of togetherness and appreciation of heritage that have helped to keep some of the state's best barbecue businesses going for several generations.

Jimmy Harvey already had 28 years of experience, including stints with Lexington barbecue pioneers Warner Stamey and Sid Weaver, when he opened his present restaurant in 1970. He's one of the biggest supporters of the Lexington Barbecue Festival, so it's no surprise that his barbecue typifies the very best Lexington has to offer. The barbecue is tender, moist, crusty-brown, and smoky (despite some recent tinkering with the cooking method). When anointed with Jimmy's fiery sauce and piled high on a soft white Flowers bun, then topped with tart barbecue slaw, this meat uplifts a barbecue sandwich from Jimmy's to lofty heights indeed.

Located just off the Interstate 85 Bypass at Exit 91 (N.C. 8/ Southmont), Jimmy's opens at 6:00 A.M. for a complete breakfast. Later in the day, in addition to the barbecue and barbecued chicken, you can choose from lots of sandwiches and several dinner plates, including fish, hamburger steak, ham, chuck-wagon steak, and ribs. No matter what you choose to eat, be sure to try the strong, sweet tea, which is mixed so well with finely crushed ice that it's *perfectly* diluted. Oh my, it's good....

John Wayne's Barbecue

601 West Fifth Avenue
Lexington, N.C. 27292
336-249-1658
Breakfast, lunch, and dinner Monday through Saturday

John Wayne's is one of those Lexington hangouts that is more popular with local residents than with out-of-towners. Located several blocks off the main drag in a low building resembling a diner, this place shows no sign of wood-burning barbecue pits, but the friendliness of the wait staff, the variety of the menu, and the pre-recorded phone message listing daily specials all win high marks from area residents. Serving a niche market, the folks operating John Wayne's probably see 90 percent of their customers on a regularly repeating basis. Considering that the Lexington barbecue hoopla must get tiring, John Wayne's probably has quite a few patrons who wouldn't care if they *never* ate barbecue again. When someone does order it, though, it's very acceptable.

Despite not serving pit-cooked pork (which makes me wonder why they mention barbecue in the name of the place), this place served me a very tender, moist barbecue sandwich, topped with some of the best-tasting coleslaw I've ever had. Barbecued chicken and barbecued beef ribs are also on the menu.

Perusing some of the daily specials, I noticed chicken pie, stew beef, pepper steak, a hamburger-steak plate, and homemade spaghetti, along with some appetizing-looking seasonal vegetables, including creamed potatoes, crowder peas, and turnip greens.

The dessert offerings vary, but they often include peach cobbler (with a biscuit-type crust), banana pudding, and homemade pound cake.

John Wayne's is open for breakfast every morning but Sunday.

For lunch or dinner, they'll fix you up with just about any kind of sandwich you might desire.

LEXINGTON BARBECUE
10 U.S. 29/70 South
Lexington, N.C. 27295
336-249-9814
Lunch and dinner Monday through Saturday
Curb service offered

The famed Lexington Barbecue sits within plain sight from the Interstate 85 Business Loop, which is also U.S. 29/70 South. It is the one place that many pilgrims would go if they could visit only one more barbecue place during their remaining time on earth.

Founder Wayne Monk learned the intricate craft of perfectly barbecuing pork shoulders at an early age by working under the tutelage of Warner Stamey, the true father of Lexington's style of pit cooking. Over the decades since he founded Lexington Barbecue in 1962, (it used to be called Lexington Barbecue #1), Monk himself has become perhaps the most widely known of all North Carolina barbecue restaurateurs.

Although the restaurant is bright and clean, there is nothing especially noteworthy about the location itself except for the clouds of white smoke from the pits, the jammed parking lot, and the cacophony of car horns from customers desiring curb service. First-time visitors often think the motorists are blowing the horns in anger. The side dishes and desserts are all expertly cooked and served, but they don't explain the mystical attraction this restaurant

The front counter stays full at "The Honeymonk."

has above all others.

The secret is that Wayne Monk worked for years to change Lexington Barbecue from a teenage hangout, which is how it began in the sixties, to a family place where the succulent barbecued pork is *the* attraction—not the sauce, the coleslaw, nor the banana pudding, but the *barbecue*. There are now probably some other restaurants that slow-roast pork shoulders over oak and hickory as well as this one does, but there is certainly no place that does it better. The fact that the restaurant's name echoes the *genre* of the cooking it represents certainly doesn't hurt. While Lexington-area residents may have favorite spots where out-of-towners don't go, Monk's place has a bigger reputation around and outside of the state than any of the other Lexington barbecue establishments. It may even be the best-known barbecue joint in the whole state, period.

Now, Rick Monk, Wayne's son, basically runs the place, with at least occasional help from Wayne's brother, his two daughters, two sons-in-law, and several cousins. Rick has his father's gift for seeing that things run smoothly and that the atmosphere remains lighthearted.

Unlike other Lexington restaurants, Lexington Barbecue does not chop the "outside brown" together with the lean meat from the inside of the shoulders. Instead, they save it for special orders. If you want to experience the closest thing to heaven on earth, order coarse, chopped, or sliced outside brown. Then, add a little of Monk's Smokehouse Sauce to the dark, chewy meat, which will already have been moistened with the house's regular dip.

Also, be aware that Wayne Monk has nearly always been called "Honey" Monk because of his reddish-brown hair. Around Lexington, the insider's way to refer to Lexington Barbecue is "Honey Monk's," "The Monk," or best of all, "The Honeymonk."

SMOKEY JOE'S BARBECUE
1101 South Main Street
Lexington, N.C. 27292
336-249-0315
Breakfast, lunch, and dinner Monday through Saturday

Located in a freestanding, flat-roofed building that has a bit of a 1950s look inside, Smokey Joe's Barbecue is right on Lexington's main drag. Old photographs from Lexington's early days as a barbecue center, along with framed Lexington Barbecue Festival posters, give some idea of the weight of tradition and expectation that rests on the shoulders of Scott and Kaffee Cope as owners of one of Lexington's premier establishments. The Copes are so dedicated to barbecue that in addition to the pits at the restaurant, they also have large brick pits at their home, where they help cook extra barbecue needed for the annual festival in October.

The day begins early with the restaurant's full breakfasts, which include eggs and hotcakes. But it's the lunch and dinner traffic that brings the place its true renown. The establishment's reputation is boosted by recommendations in both *Southern Living* and *USA Today*, to say nothing of word-of-mouth praise from hundreds of thousands of barbecue lovers.

As the sign says at Smokey Joe's, the barbecue is "pit cooked the ole fashioned way." While many Lexington-area barbecue places can make that claim, I believe Smokey Joe's has, hands down, the most tender slow-roasted pork shoulder in town—as well as the sweetest iced tea I've ever tasted.

I like to order coarse-chopped barbecue, which usually arrives cut into cubes roughly one-inch square. At Smokey Joe's, these moist, flavorful bites, lightly kissed with the restaurant's peppery dip and subtly flavored by wood smoke and the steam from fat melting onto coals, melt onto your tongue without being chewed at all. The meat is so tender and enjoyable that a well-balanced barbecue slaw and crisp hush puppies go almost unnoticed.

Smokey Joe's pit-cooks barbecued chicken on Thursday, Friday, and Saturday and offers whole, pit-cooked pork shoulders for $4.00 per pound. Rather than buying several pounds of chopped barbecue to feed a large group, I'd suggest buying a whole shoulder, which will feed around 15 people, and chopping and seasoning it yourself, perhaps with some of Smokey Joe's delicious dip, which is also for sale to take out. Remember to salt the chopped meat lightly before moistening it with the sauce.

Southern Barbecue

907 Winston Road (N.C. 8 North)
Lexington, N.C. 27295
336-248-4528
Curb service is offered

Second location:
Southern Barbecue Too
10361 N.C. 8 South
Southmont, N.C. 27351
336-798-2300

Both locations: Breakfast, lunch, and dinner Tuesday through Sunday

Southern Barbecue's original location, which is near downtown Lexington, is a great little place. It has one of the most exhaustive outdoor signs listing daily specials that I've ever seen. Except for certain items that are available all the time, you eat according to the day of the week here. The place opened in the 1960s as Smiley's. Although the name has changed, it'll still keep you smiling, for sure.

The barbecue is the real, pit-cooked thing, with lots of flavor. The serving I had was not quite cooked to the falling-apart stage but served swimming in tangy dip, it was still very good. The barbecued chicken, however, *was* falling off the bone. It was pink from the wood smoke and wonderful. The red slaw was a little chunkier in consistency than some and was adroitly seasoned.

Next to barbecue, Southern specializes in hot dogs. They are supposedly the best in Lexington, and there are always plenty of people either waiting in their cars for curb service or buzzing around the register waiting for their 'dogs to go. One customer came in and bought 20 at one whack while I was there.

For daily choices, on Monday and Tuesday, you can enjoy chili beans and homemade soup, while Wednesday brings stew beef, white beans, and cabbage. Thursday's the day for Salisbury steak, okra & tomatoes, and pintos; while Friday, Saturday, and Sunday are proudly set aside for Southern's delicious pit-cooked barbecued chicken. Creamed potatoes, white and red slaw, and potato salad are available every day.

Both the location near downtown and Southern Barbecue Too, the new High Rock Lake outpost in Southmont, also serve a mean pork-skin sandwich.

Not too many out-of-town pilgrims know about Southern Barbecue, but plenty of locals know what's what, and they keep this place busy.

SPEEDY'S BARBECUE
1317 Winston Road (N.C. 8 North)
Lexington, N.C. 27295
336-248-2410
Lunch and dinner Monday through Saturday

Speedy's has a mysterious attraction I can't quite figure out. After Lexington Barbecue, it's definitely the most popular barbecue joint in Lexington, particularly with local residents, *despite* the fact that it no longer pit-cooks its barbecue.

Don't get me wrong: I've never had anything other than tasty, well-prepared food at Speedy's. In fact, if you leave much on your plate, a concerned waitress will follow you to the cash register and ask what was wrong. But in a town like Lexington, with its reputation for wood-cooked barbecue, cooking on electric pits and claiming, as Speedy's does, to have not only "Lexington's Finest Barbecue," but "The Best Barbecue in the USA" takes a lot of nerve. This is especially true in a place that *had* been pit cooking since it originally opened as Tussy's back in the 1930s. In fact, the meat was pit-cooked right on up through Speedy Lohr's ownership and up until the latest owners took over. Current proprietors Roy and Boyd Dunn are obviously brimming with confidence, and somehow they've managed to put together a blend of atmosphere, service, and whatever else to keep their

Speedy's Barbecue in Lexington has a 1950s atmosphere.
DAN ROUTH PHOTOGRAPHY

large parking lot packed. They give Wayne and Rick Monk of Lexington Barbecue a run for their money—without a single whiff of the aroma of wood smoke.

In fact, I do have to give the barbecue at Speedy's pretty high marks. My coarse-chopped tray contained beautiful chunks of lean, tender meat that was very fresh tasting, albeit without the pit flavor that I so enjoy. The dip is a very spicy-hot mixture, with a definite tomato taste, not unlike tomato soup with peppery heat. The barbecue slaw had more of a kick than most I've tasted (I like it hot!), but the hush puppies seemed to be those uniformly shaped, relatively tasteless frozen things that so many places are turning to. 'Pup lovers, speak out!

Speedy's has hot dogs, sandwiches, and some plate dinners (including fish, country ham, and hamburger steak), and the burgers are supposed to be very good. In fact, one lady spent several minutes describing the "divine" burger she had recently enjoyed there.

Oddly enough, there was no banana pudding or cobbler for dessert—just mediocre store-bought pies on the menu and a selection of B&G fried pies and cellophane-wrapped honey buns up at the register.

What Speedy's *did* have, though, was three—*three*—dining rooms packed with customers. Somebody's doing something right.

Tar Heel Q
6835 U.S. 64 West
Lexington, N.C. 27295
336-787-4550
Breakfast, lunch, and dinner Monday through Saturday

Established in 1984, Tar Heel Q is located in an attractive tan stucco building with gray trim, beside a Texaco station on a rural stretch of U.S. 64. Out back, the large brick pit and neatly stacked woodpile are ample evidence that the owners intend to compete seriously for their share of the barbecue market in the Lexington area, despite being a little off the beaten track.

Considering that this rural restaurant is seven miles or so west of downtown Lexington, almost at the Yadkin River, I was surprised to find it crowded halfway through a Saturday afternoon. However, my surprise at the number of customers at 3:00 P.M. evaporated once my order was brought to the table.

Advertising "old-style pit barbecue," Tar Heel Q seems to

deliver the goods as well as any place in the area. My order of coarse-chopped, outside-brown barbecue was absolutely superb. It was crisp and chewy on the surface, reddish-colored from wood smoke, tender and full of flavor. The sauce was a little milder and a little thicker than many of the local "dips," but it complemented the meat to perfection. The barbecue slaw had just the right amount of bite to it (white slaw is available, as well), while the hush puppies were just the way I like them best: tiny and crisp, with a pure cornmeal flavor and only a hint of sugar.

Lexington-area residents in the know speak highly of both the barbecued chicken and the baby back ribs at Tar Heel Q, although I didn't have the opportunity to try either. The chicken is available Thursday through Saturday, while the ribs are a once-a-week treat on Wednesday nights.

The locals also speak highly of the breakfasts at Tar Heel Q, which begin at 6:00 A.M. (Actually, I have a hard time imagining a meal here that doesn't include some of that wonderfully smoked pork barbecue.) A complete selection of sandwiches, salads, and dinner plates is also available.

Tar Heel Q is located on U.S. 64, 6.1 miles west of the U.S. 52 Bypass, near the Thousand Trails Campground and just past Reeds Crossroads.

WHITLEY'S BARBECUE

3664 N.C. 8 South
Lexington, N.C. 27292
336-357-2364
Breakfast, lunch, and dinner Monday through Saturday

Whitley's Barbecue does a good job of preparing just about any kind of food you might want, including pit-cooked barbecue. While it isn't one of the best-known barbecue stops in Lexington—at least for out-of-towners—it has its own devoted clientele of locals, many of who are no doubt trying to get away from the *turistas* anyhow.

Located one mile south of Interstate 85 on N.C. 8, this flat-topped brick building with the hip roof and the Formica-topped booths is unremarkable in appearance, but the staff is friendly. More importantly, there's a fresh-looking woodpile out back to feed the barbecue pits.

I ordered a coarse-chopped barbecue tray and found the meat lightly flavored with wood smoke, tender, and really quite good. The barbecue slaw that accompanied it was very tangy. It was so finely chopped that it seemed almost puréed, but I didn't consider this a drawback. The hush puppies were extremely even in shape, which led me to believe they may have been frozen, but as much as I hate to admit it, they tasted fine. Still, convenience isn't everything, and I firmly believe restaurants doggone well ought to continue taking the trouble to make their own hush puppies.

Besides a regular breakfast menu, Whitley's has several daily specials. On Monday and Tuesday, Whitley's offers a meat-and-three-vegetable plate with hamburger steak, country ham, and their signature fried chicken as the meat choices. Wednesday is the day for the homemade spaghetti special, while country-style steak is featured on Thursday. Seafood entrées are available, and the house special barbecued chicken is prepared each week on Thursday, Friday, and Saturday only. The restaurant's sandwich selection includes the "Whitburger," which sounds pretty good.

All in all, Whitley's offers a safe, predictable, middle-of-the-road barbecue experience, with no breathtaking highs or terrifying lows. And that ain't a bad deal.

HOWARD'S BARBECUE
100 South Main Street
Lillington, N.C. 27546
910-893-4571
Lunch and dinner Tuesday through Friday
Lunch only on Saturday

Established in 1978, Howard's Barbecue now has a relatively new location on the opposite side of the U.S. 421 bridge from its original spot. The good news is that Howard's still overlooks the Cape Fear River in Lillington. The newer location has a trendy brick-red-and-green color scheme, framed black-and-white prints of old Lillington scenes, a glassed-in porch, and a kid's play area. But next to the barbecue itself, the most important thing about Howard's is the beautiful river view.

After noticing no pit or woodpile, I still kept a very open mind. I was pleased to find that the eastern-style barbecue was very tasty and juicy, obviously hand-chopped, and not a bit dried out. This was a pleasant surprise since some eastern 'cue that's chopped by machine has an almost mushy consistency. Howard's barbecue is a bit on the hot side for some palates, with visible red pepper flakes and tiny bits of fat chopped in to carry the flavor. It's seasoned so well that it really doesn't need additional amounts of Howard's sauce, which is basically a straight eastern-style mix of vinegar, salt, and black and red pepper, with no sugar added.

The sweet, white coleslaw, which has no mustard, complements the salty, spicy barbecue perfectly, especially on a sandwich. The smooth stewed potatoes, which are cooked with onions, are also a perfect side dish. The signature hush puppies at Howard's are curly creations, shaped more or less like pretzels. They're very sweet, like the iced tea, but when combined with the peppery barbecue and savory spuds, the sweet sides and tea all help create a nice balance. When I visited, I only intended to try a few small bites, having eaten another meal a short time before, but I ended up eating my entire dinner. (This seems to be a big and frequent problem for me.)

I also found room to try Howard's Brunswick stew, which is appetizing but very unusual. The stew has lots of chopped chicken and pork, potatoes, diced tomatoes, and whole-kernel corn, but there are no butter beans. The mixture resembles a sweet, hearty chicken-tomato-and-corn chowder, rather than the more thickened stew you find most often.

The restful scenery and the well-prepared barbecue and fixin's at Howard's make it a really nice place to stop.

SPEARS BARBECUE & GRILL
Intersection of U.S. 221 and N.C. 183
Linville Falls, N.C. 28647
828-765-2658
Lunch and dinner daily May through October
Dinner on Friday; lunch and dinner Saturday and Sunday, November through April

This fairly upscale restaurant is under the same ownership as the adjacent Linville Falls Lodge. Spears Barbecue & Grill offers wood-smoked barbecue but, paradoxically, the rest of the menu is the very antithesis of the fare you'd expect in a barbecue establishment.

Located only a few yards from a spot where the boundaries of Burke, McDowell, and Avery Counties intersect, the restaurant, which is actually in Burke County, is an attractive wood-shingle and stone structure with a hip roof, painted in gray and green trim. Booths line the side of a long, narrow front room, which opens into an attractive main dining room with dark-green and brick-red accents. Paneled wainscoting, framed black-and-white prints of mountain life, and a stained-glass window depicting waterfowl create an atmosphere of quiet elegance. For those who aren't seeking sauce and smoke, other entrées include rainbow trout, grilled salmon with cream sauce, steaks, and salads. There is also a respectable wine list.

But out behind this quiet, tasteful oasis is a screened-in pit house containing a no-nonsense iron smoker. Here Boston butts, the upper half of the pork shoulder, are smoked with hickory and apple wood for fourteen hours. The meat is cooked in a smoke chamber offset from the firebox, rather than directly over the coals, as is the custom with traditional North Carolina barbecue. This meat isn't chopped or "pulled," as it is with Memphis-style barbecue. Instead it is served in thin slices, which are then cut into smaller pieces. This style is reminiscent of the highly regarded Ridgewood Barbecue, outside Bluff City, Tennessee, near Bristol. Spears is the only other place I've seen barbecue cut up this way.

The meat is very tender, with a brown, crusty exterior and a pleasant smoky flavor. However, it was difficult to tell how much of that flavor came from the cooking process and how much from the sauce, which contains smoke flavoring, tomato paste, mustard, and molasses. The meat was, by far, the most memorable item on my plate compared to the hush puppies, bland coleslaw, and baked beans, but that is as it should be. I give the owners high marks for taking the trouble to turn out real, wood-cooked barbecue, albeit in a slightly different style, so far from the barbecue heartland. Like the cool temperatures and the mountain scenery, it's a refreshing change of pace.

BACKCOUNTRY BARBEQUE
4014 Linwood-Southmont Road
Linwood, N.C. 27299
336-956-1696
Breakfast, lunch, and dinner Monday through Saturday
Lunch and dinner on Sunday

Owner Doug Cook must have a thing for homely, ramshackle buildings (see the Cook's Barbecue entry). His Backcountry Barbeque, housed in a squat building with a spindly tin-roofed overhang, looks like a cross between a country store that's fallen on hard times and a place where dogfights might be held. Located well out in the country, the place sits across the highway from a furniture plant and in front of an old barn absolutely overflowing with quartered hardwood logs. Even more revealing than the logs are several large ash piles out behind the restaurant, some of which are still smoking. All that wood and all those burned-out coals are signs that someone here is doing some serious *barbecuing*. Beside the restaurant is the largest pecan tree I've ever seen in my life, with windfall pecans all over the ground. Although they sell plastic bags of shelled pecans inside the restaurant, I'm told they don't come from this tree. I just accept the fact that this place is a little quirky.

Backcountry Barbecue is an old-fashioned pit-cooker in Linwood, near Lexington.
DAN ROUTH PHOTOGRAPHY

A small sign on the front of the building reads: "Backcountry: Breakfast—BBQ—Burgers—Steaks." Inside, there are only about ten tables. On the wall hangs an absolutely huge picture of the Linwood Fire Department Station 41 and its personnel, who, come to think of it, are the buddies you want when you're dealing with smoke, fire, and burning fat every day. Even so, it's still a *really* big picture for such a small room. Indian pottery and framed prints of western scenes also decorate the tiny restaurant, a circumstance explained by the fact that Cook is an absentee owner who now spends most of his time in Colorado.

What can I say about the barbecue at Backcountry except that it's incredible? Dark reddish-brown, lean, moist, chewy, tender, and robustly flavored by the hardwood pit, the pork is served with a delicious, fiery dip, which is served warm. The meat is also served with a terrific barbecue slaw, which has a lingering peppery aftertaste. This restaurant serves the same small, round hush puppies as does Cook's Barbecue, and they're as irresistible as fresh popcorn shrimp.

What do you have when you're not eating barbecue at Backcountry? Well, refer to the sign out front: breakfast, sandwiches (burgers, mostly, although the pork-skin sandwiches are always in high demand), and sirloin steaks—that's the only cut of steak they prepare. The overwhelming favorite among local customers (and one of the best food deals on the planet) is the 20-ounce sirloin, which comes with two trips to the salad bar, two baked potatoes, and rolls for two—easily enough food for three—for $17.99. I *love* this place.

To get there, take Exit 88 (Linwood Exit) from Interstate 85. Go south on Linwood-Southmont Road one mile to the restaurant, which is located on the right side. Be careful—you could easily drive past without paying any attention to this ugly duckling.

FUZZY'S

U.S. 220 Business
Madison, N.C. 27025
336-427-4130
Lunch and dinner daily

Because of its relatively out-of-the-way location in the Rockingham County community of Madison, Fuzzy's hasn't enjoyed the visibility that many other top North Carolina barbecue spots have experienced. However, it *is* well known to locals, Triad-area residents, and travelers who head up U.S. 220 North toward Martinsville and Roanoke. If you're headed in that direction, detour on to U.S. 220 Business and go into downtown Madison for a Fuzzy's fix.

It isn't that the place hasn't had a shot at the big time. Both conservative radio personality Barry Farber, who lived in nearby Greensboro, and magazine/TV model Zacki Murphy, who was raised in Hillsborough, tried on different occasions to import Fuzzy's barbecue, which was "flash frozen," to New York City for sale. Although the North Carolina delicacy was initially well received, a cutthroat business climate made both ventures unsustainable.

Fuzzy's serves honest-to-goodness, pit-cooked pork barbecue: shoulders for chopped 'cue, hams for sliced. The sauce is thicker and sweeter than what is served in most of the other barbecue establishments in the Piedmont, and the chopped barbecue is more heavily moistened with sauce than most any other I've encountered, with the exception of Dillard's in Durham. Don't be put off by that, because it's terrific stuff.

You'll get a kick out of the hush puppies (or more properly, the hush *puppy*) at Fuzzy's. Because the batter is squeezed from a pastry bag into the hot oil in a long continuous strand, each customer gets one more or less pretzel-shaped pup.

On Wednesdays, the place serves up some of the best pinto beans you'll ever eat, and every seat in the place is likely to be filled with someone who's enjoying a bowlful.

Fuzzy's homemade banana pudding, which is served warm and topped with a beautifully browned layer of meringue, is a rare, incredibly tasty treat. It's such a treat, in fact, that the restaurant is likely to run out before the close of business each day.

You should be aware that there is now a Fuzzy's wholesale operation producing mass quantities of cooked pork, Brunswick stew, and chili. I'm unable to say whether the quality of these foods matches that of the offerings at the restaurant in Madison.

A&M GRILL
401 East Center Street (U.S. 70 East)
Mebane, N.C. 27302
919-563-3721
Lunch and dinner Monday through Saturday

If I were assigning ratings, A&M Grill, which has been in business since 1948, would rate five out of five little pigs, stars, sauce bottles, or whatever other icon we might devise to indicate absolutely excellent barbecue. Located within the city limits of Mebane, but some 100 yards into Orange County, A&M Grill turns out what's unquestionably the best pit-cooked barbecue in the Greensboro to Hillsborough stretches of Interstate 40/85 and U.S. 70.

Ironically, when I first started producing features about

Mebane's A&M Grill on U.S. 70

outstanding North Carolina barbecue restaurants for UNC-TV, A&M's owners wouldn't allow me to come and do a story. Even though it would have meant some free publicity, they weren't any too polite about declining, either. When I first approached them with the idea, I think they assumed I was trying to sell them something. Although I explained a number of times that there was no charge involved, they were unmoved, telling me, "We just really don't want to talk to anyone."

So just to have some fun, we ended up doing what we referred to—tongue in cheek—as an "undercover barbecue" report, complete with dark glasses and a miniature hidden camera.

With no hard feelings whatsoever, I'm happy to report that A&M Grill doesn't have time to leave the serious work of cooking great barbecue long enough to fool around with any bothersome TV guys. This is obvious when you walk into the small, original dining room and hear the hollow *thunk* of barbecue being hand-chopped. The place has proved so popular that a newer, larger room has been added. Out back, the brick pits, chimneys, and a large pile of split wood let you know immediately that you've arrived at an old-fashioned, uncompromising, pit-cooking barbecue place.

I ordered a small, sliced tray, which means just barbecue, coleslaw, and hush puppies (no potatoes). It turned out to contain an absolutely huge serving of the "pig pickin' " (or pulled) style meat. The pork was falling-apart tender, with a robust smoky flavor. It was practically as good as it ever gets.

As I've explained elsewhere, eastern North Carolina coleslaw is white or yellow, moistened with mayonnaise or mustard, while Lexington-style "barbecue" slaw (also known as "red slaw") contains vinegar, sugar, ketchup, and red and black pepper. Orange and Alamance Counties are in a sort of in-between, nether region. They follow the Piedmont practice of cooking pork shoulders rather than whole hogs, but they don't feel quite comfortable serving barbecue slaw. (The dividing line for Lexington-style slaw seems to begin around Greensboro.) A&M Grill and a few Alamance County joints solve this split-personality problem by serving *pink* slaw, which contains both mayonnaise and ketchup. It actually tastes as if it's been dressed with Thousand Island dressing.

The Brunswick stew, which A&M prepares on Tuesday and Saturday only, is quite good. It contains both diced potatoes and chunks of tomatoes, rather than tomato sauce or purée.

A larger establishment next door, the A&M Grill and Bar, opens at 5:00 P.M. It specializes in steaks, prime rib, and such. For my money, the original barbecue place is where it's happening.

HUEY'S RESTAURANT AND OYSTER BAR

7601 U.S. 70
Mebane, N.C. 27302
919-563-8900
Lunch and dinner Tuesday through Sunday

The Huey name has been well known for barbecue in the Mebane and Burlington area for a number of years. Huey's Restaurant and Oyster Bar is actually located in Orange County, but it's not far from the Alamance County line. As its name implies, Huey's offers a full-service menu and an oyster bar. However, barbecue is an important, if not exactly prominent, item on the bill of fare.

The menu at Huey's promises "hickory *smoked* barbecue and ribs," but the pork is cooked on an electric smoker, which contains smoldering wood chunks, rather than on an old-fashioned pit. I think this actually makes a lot of sense at a restaurant that features so many other items besides barbecue.

The chopped pork is extremely moist and tender, with a good texture that is not too finely chopped. It is brought to the table already doused with a liberal application of Huey's tangy, tomato-based sauce. Sweet white coleslaw and very light, crunchy hush puppies balance the barbecue perfectly. The overall taste experience is very pleasant.

Huey's also serves some of the best Brunswick stew I've ever had in the Piedmont. This is a little surprising, since I've encountered some other stews in the area that were sketchy, to say the least. Huey's stew would qualify anywhere as a very genuine version of this dish. It contains what I stubbornly consider to be the correct ingredients, and it is reminiscent of the best of the Brunswick stews of the coastal-plain region.

In addition to barbecue and pork ribs, Huey's features a large daily buffet and salad bar, seafood, chicken, steaks, and a good choice of sandwiches.

Look for an attractive brick building with dark-brown trim and dormer windows built into the roofline. It's on the right as you travel from Hillsborough toward Mebane on U.S. 70.

DEANO'S BARBECUE
140 North Clement Street
Mocksville, N.C. 27028
336-751-5820
Lunch and dinner Tuesday through Saturday

Dean Allen, proprietor of Deano's in downtown Mocksville, earned his spurs working for two of the best-known barbecue experts in Davie County: the late Buck Miller, who owned Buck's Barbecue, and the late Odell "Bony" Hendrix, who built Hendrix Barbecue on U.S. 64. Allen actually ran both places for a number of years after their owners retired, so his barbecue credentials are solid.

Deano's is located in a new building, which can send a shiver of apprehension running up the spine of someone searching for old-time barbecue. But never fear—the place has a real, honest-to-goodness pit and a reassuring pile of hardwood outside. His place has a nice, natural wood exterior and a pleasant front porch, equipped with picnic tables and rocking chairs (a touch you would think more barbecue restaurants would consider).

Inside, old advertising signs, appliances, and novelties are reminders of the 1940s and 1950s, the golden age of North Carolina barbecue. There's an old Merita bread screen door, an antique

Dr. Pepper cold-drink box, a Sinclair gas pump emblazoned with the silhouette of a dinosaur, and an old soda fountain.

Deano's seems to specialize in young, friendly waitresses with something of a gift of gab. Their sunny dispositions are a welcome touch in an age when so many of their counterparts either refuse to make eye contact (a defense against having to acknowledge your existence) or deliver a clear, though unspoken, message that they dislike their jobs and would prefer to be somewhere else.

Deano's barbecue is very finely chopped and very mild, albeit with a distinctive wood-cooked flavor. Personally, I found it a bit more interesting with a little Texas Pete added, but as they say, it's easier to add it than to take it out. I selected tasty homemade French fries and a nice peach cobbler to go with my meal. Overall, I would rate the food quite highly.

That high rating goes as well for an unusual offering at Deano's: the bison burger. Bison meat is supposed to be quite a bit healthier than beef because of its lower fat and cholesterol content, but it is a bit drier. I tried a burger with lettuce, tomato, and mayonnaise (the latter of which overrides the health benefits, I suppose) and found it very enjoyable. I was surprised to find the bison burger priced at only three dollars, compared to two dollars for a regular hamburger.

Deano's also features daily specials, which include barbecued chicken on Fridays and occasional offerings of chicken and dumplings, barbecued stew beef, and pinto beans and cornbread.

To reach this pleasant restaurant, take Exit 170 from Interstate 40, then turn left and follow U.S. 601 South for 3 miles to its intersection with N.C. 158 East (North Main Street). Turn left on to N.C. 158 and go through the town square and past one traffic light. Turn left on to Church Street. Deano's is on the left on the corner of Church and Clement Streets.

Hendrix Barbecue is a wood-burner on U.S. 64, east of Mocksville.

HENDRIX BARBECUE
2837 U.S. 64 East
Mocksville, N.C. 27028
336-998-8230
Breakfast, lunch, and dinner Tuesday through Friday
Breakfast and lunch on Saturday

Hendrix Barbecue is the kind of place that cross-country barbecue explorers like me dream of stumbling across. It's a tiny takeout-only place on a rural stretch of U.S. 64 west of Lexington. It's actually located in the community of Fork, though the mailing address is Mocksville, which is located a few miles farther.

If Hendrix Barbecue were located in eastern North Carolina, it would be called a "bobbycue stand." Except for a picnic table in the yard and a couple of plastic chairs in the minuscule waiting area outside the takeout window, customers basically stand and wait, then stand while they eat their barbecue. The group of locals I encountered one Saturday chose to stand around the tailgate of a pickup out front while they shot the breeze, munched their sandwiches, and washed them down with canned drinks from a cooler on the truck.

Odell "Bony" Hendrix built the place in 1968, and his grandson, Kevin, runs it today.

Odell must have been well known locally, because I noticed his picture hanging on the wall of a Mocksville barbecue restaurant run by one of his former employees. You have to wonder why "Bony" built such a small facility, but Kevin says cheerfully that he "don't want no big place." In truth, Hendrix Barbecue seems perfect exactly as it is. All the really important elements are here: a large woodpile, a real pit, and a wood-chopping block with a six-inch-deep bowl-shaped depression worn into it (Kevin says the bottom of the block is similarly worn). All these signs indicate that a lot of good barbecue has been cooked and chopped on the premises.

I enjoyed a chopped sandwich with barbecue slaw that can only be described as spectacular. The meat was smoky and exceptionally tender, dressed with a sweet, Lexington-style dip that enhanced the pork's natural sweetness and left behind a pleasant, peppery aftertaste. The hamburgers, foot-long hot dogs, and grilled cheese sandwiches all looked freshly made and appetizing, and the wall-mounted menu board indicated that breakfast is available as well.

Hendrix Barbecue is located on U.S. 64 about 1.2 miles west of the intersection with N.C. 801. This intersection is also the location of historic Fork Baptist Church, organized in 1793.

THE RED PIG BARBECUE HOUSE

Intersection of N.C. 801 and U.S. 601
Mocksville, N.C. 27028
336-284-4650
Breakfast, lunch, and dinner daily

The Red Pig is the last holdout at "Greasy Corner," the intersection of N.C. 801 and U.S. 601, located south of Mocksville. This spot, which is actually known as Davie Crossroads, was once home to several barbecue joints. The Red Pig Barbecue House is the only survivor and it's hard to miss. Beside the long tan-and-brown building are a large, eye-catching barbecue pit and a yard filled with bundles of split hardwood slabs bound with metal strips. So far, so good.

An inviting, comfortable interior features large front and back rooms. The front dining area is decorated with shelves holding old kitchen jars, farm implements, and various kitchen gadgets. The comfortable booths along the walls and in the room's center are painted a soothing dark-and-light-green combination.

During the rather long wait for my simple barbecue tray (hmmm—I noticed a couple of others waiting quite awhile, too), I had time to check out the lengthy menu. There's a large selection of sandwiches, including a local favorite—fried bologna. You can find just about any dinner plate you might desire, including chicken, shrimp, and hamburger steak. There are also quite a few daily specials. The Saturday I was there, the menu offered country-style steak, fried chicken, baked ham, and chicken livers, with sides of pintos, creamed potatoes, baked apples, white beans, and beets. They also serve breakfast.

When my order finally arrived, I found it *well* worth the wait. My chopped barbecue was exceptionally tender, smoky-tasting, mild and sweet, although the sauce was just a little too thick and too much on the red side for my taste. (It's my firm conviction that nearly without exception, the sauce grows thicker the further west one travels.) The barbecue, which is cooked seven days a week, was slightly mild to my personal taste, but a dash of hot sauce made it perfect. All in all, this has to be described as really good pit-cooked barbecue.

The impressive chopped pork was accompanied by a very coarsely chopped barbecue slaw, which was mild but tasty. Rounding out the order were excellent, golf-ball-size hush puppies, which had a clean, not too sweet, cornmeal flavor and were very light and crisp on the outside.

The Red Pig seems like a relaxing local hangout, with familiar, unpretentious surroundings and a menu full of "comfort foods." It has survived at "Greasy Corner" while its competitors faded, and that alone makes it worth adding to your list of barbecue places to visit.

BRANCH'S BARBECUE
713 Red Hill Road
Mount Olive, N.C. 28365
919-658-2031
Lunch and dinner on Friday and Saturday only

I hesitate to even mention this wonderful place, because I would really like it to remain what it has been since 1962: one of the best-kept secrets in eastern North Carolina. Let me stress from the beginning that Branch's is also really, r-e-a-l-l-y hard to find. Only

Friday and Saturday lunch hours are busy at Branch's Barbecue near Mount Olive.

the truly pure of heart will be able to make all the correct turns and keep an accurate eye on distances.

Please don't bother trying to find Branch's if you expect it to be anything other than a very modest, rural eatery. It has something of a jumbled interior decor and fairly unsophisticated kitchen arrangements. However, if you're willing to mind your manners, keep a low profile, speak softly, and try to fit in with the local patrons, what you'll discover is one of the most delightful traditional dining experiences in North Carolina.

Branch's is a genuine rural "bobbycue stand," serving lunch and dinner on Friday and Saturday only. The simple furnishings consist of three booths and a takeout counter.

Since 1962, Norman Branch, a friendly, outgoing black man, and other members of the extended Branch family have operated this establishment. Out behind the roadside restaurant, you'll find piles of hardwood and fifty-five-gallon barrels, which are used to burn split wood down to glowing coals. This process testifies to Branch's commitment to cooking the whole hog in the authentic eastern North Carolina manner.

And what wonderful barbecue it is! The chopped pork is definitely served eastern style—infused with smoke flavor, chopped fine, and accented by a wonderfully seasoned, vinegar-based sauce with just a hint of sweetness. Along with this exceptional barbecue, you get a tasty piece of fried pork skin. Recommended side dishes include a perfect, white coleslaw; green beans with bits of bacon; and the best country-style cabbage you've ever tasted.

But wait, there's more. You can order servings of light, yet rich chicken and dumplings; hearty stew beef over rice; and spicy, smooth sweet-potato pie. All of this heavenly food is accompanied by mild, nectar-like sweet tea.

With perfect confidence, Norman informs me that each Friday, the place also serves the "best fried fish in North Carolina." He serves flounder and trout fillets, while spots are cooked with the bones intact for peak flavor.

The steady parade of local patrons that wait for takeout orders pay no attention to the kitchen's eclectic mixture of commercial and home-style pots and pans. When I visited, several customers went outside to enjoy picnicking under the pine trees and to watch the comings and goings of the other patrons. Several patrons presented me with tongue-in-cheek warnings about not ruining Branch's by "letting too many people know about it."

If you're coming from Mount Olive to Branch's, take N.C. 55 east to N.C. 111. Turn south on N.C. 111 and go 2.5 miles to Zion Church Road. Turn right on Zion Church Road, then make an immediate left onto Bennett Bridge Road. Go 6.8 miles, passing through White Flash and Scott's Store, until the road dead-ends at

Red Hill Road. Turn right on to Red Hill Road. On this road, you will travel 3 miles before reaching Branch's. The building is located on the right.

Since none of us want Branch's to become a victim of its own success, let's all agree to slip in and out of the place with little fanfare. We can all sort of keep the whole deal under our hats.

WHITLEY'S BAR-B-QUE
315 Beechwood Boulevard (N.C. 11)
Murfreesboro, N.C. 27855
252-398-4884
Lunch and dinner Tuesday through Sunday

This noteworthy restaurant started out in 1963 as a weekend, carry-out barbecue business on the Whitley family farm. It was located down a dirt road, less than a mile from Murfreesboro. Later, N.C. 11 split the farm in half, putting the business on a main artery. That turned what had been a sideline into a full-time restaurant that's now one of the most popular barbecue places in the northeastern area of the state.

Whitley's is located in an attractive single-story building, with light-gray clapboard siding and black shutters. Landscaped grounds surround the building, which has a view of a peaceful pond from one of its two dining rooms. Inside, a white cinder-block main room has plain, unfinished wood floors, a long counter, and wooden tables. A beautiful old roll-top desk and an antique cold-drink box add decorative touches. The side dining room, which was added later, is paneled in warm knotty pine.

Ruth Whitley, daughter of the original owner, has turned the site of the farm's old chicken house into an open-sided party shelter, equipped with a rest room, bar, refrigerator-freezer, gas cooker, and tables and chairs. Nicely landscaped and located in a wooded grove some 200 yards from the restaurant building, the shelter seems to be a prime spot to rent for private parties.

The barbecue at Whitley's is quite good. It's relatively coarsely hand-chopped and well seasoned, although without the telltale flavor that would indicate it had been cooked on a wood-burning pit. Along with the barbecue, I had tasty, mustard-based slaw; authentic Brunswick stew (perhaps not quite as thick as some); and deep-fried corn sticks, rather than hush puppies. Surprisingly, Whitley's barbecue sauce is almost a Lexington-style dip. It's vinegar-based, but thick and somewhat sweet.

For dessert, I chose scrumptious homemade banana ice cream, which was as good as any I've ever had. I was also tempted by Bernice Jenkins's homemade Milky Way cake, because I was told every one of these cakes contains 11 whole Milky Way candy bars. Bernice, incidentally, has been with Whitley's since 1974.

For travelers finding themselves in the Ahoskie-Murfreesboro area, or for those heading toward Tidewater Virginia along U.S. 158, Whitley's is a worthwhile stop. It's located less than a mile south of Murfreesboro on N.C. 11.

The late John Moore's son Tommy (left) and grandson Bryan now operate Moore's Olde Tyme Barbecue in New Bern.

MOORE'S OLDE TYME BARBECUE

3711 U.S. 17 South
New Bern, N.C. 28562
252-638-3937
Lunch and dinner Monday through Saturday

After passing a string of chain restaurants on New Bern's Clarendon Boulevard (U.S. 17 South), it's good to smell the wood smoke and see the no-nonsense building that houses Moore's Barbecue. Moore's has what must be the biggest woodpile in the entire state. The place actually looks like a sawmill. Even though the barbecue at Moore's is now cooked part of the time over wood coals and part of the time in an electric pit, the process still produces barbecue that's worth going out of the way for.

Actually, even though Moore's has been at its present location since 1973, there were six previous locations around New Bern. Owner Tommy Moore, who now runs the place with his son Bryan, says his father, Big John Moore, started in the barbecue business in 1945 before there *was* a location at all. The elder Moore borrowed thirty-five dollars to buy a pig and paid someone to cook it over a pit dug into the ground. He had the idea that after he sold the barbecue and paid off the cook, he could buy another pig and keep going. The scheme worked, although Moore was nearly run out of business right off the bat when the pig escaped before Moore could get it slaughtered. Fortunately for us all, he caught and cooked that first porker, sold the barbecue, and bought another. He plowed the profits back into the business until he was able to open up shop in a converted gas station. Try to imagine someone building a respectable business from the ground up that way today.

Moore's has always been a modest, no-frills kind of place. The kitchen and order counter are in the center and plain dining rooms, where customers carry their own food, are located on either side. In 2002, Tommy Moore expanded one of the dining rooms considerably, but the place is still fairly basic. It's just the spot to enjoy honest-to-goodness, whole-hog barbecue.

Moore's serves up its pork in little rectangular Styrofoam trays. The meat is very finely chopped and tender, with tiny bits of crisp skin mixed in. The sauce is a typical eastern vinegar-and-red pepper mixture blended for today's tastes. Unlike the traditional eastern sauce of bygone years, the sauce now has some sugar added to cut the acidity. The chopped 'cue is served with finely chopped white coleslaw, which is seasoned mostly with vinegar and sugar. The hush puppies look and taste exactly as puffs of fried corn bread should: perfectly light, golden brown, and not too sweet. All of the foods I ordered seemed to go together extraordinarily well, creating a perfect balance.

The place is also well known for its seafood, which is mainly shrimp, flounder, and trout. It's also known for its fried chicken, although several regulars told me that the barbecued chicken is superb, too. Every Saturday, ribs are prepared and served with the thick, red sauce that now seems to be expected with this particular cut of meat.

In 1988, Moore's was included in a book that detailed the authors' picks of the top 100 barbecue places in America. While all such lists, including this one, are somewhat arbitrary, you can bet that Moore's should stay on your must-go list until you have a chance to taste for yourself.

ALLEN & SON BAR-B-QUE
5650 U.S. 15-501
Pittsboro, N.C. 27312
919-542-2294
Lunch and dinner Monday through Saturday

Established by Henry Hearne in 1950, this place became the first location of Allen & Son Bar-B-Que after James Allen purchased it from Hearne in the early 1960s. Recently it's often been referred to as the "other" location, particularly since James's son Keith began attracting a lot of customers to his Chapel Hill "Allen & Son" by insisting—unlike this restaurant—on continuing to cook barbecue only over pure hickory coals.

Although it has a Pittsboro mailing address, this place is actually located in the community of Bynum, halfway between Chapel Hill and Pittsboro. It is now leased to Jimmy and Rhonda Stubbs. Since the pork shoulders are now roasted on a gas-fired pit, the firebox of the old, original pit is used only for burning trash. Still, the place has its share of enthusiastic supporters and was listed as a top spot for barbecue in a 2001 issue of *Travel* magazine.

The takeout window, which faces U.S. 15-501, is where much of the action takes place, especially among customers ordering barbecue sandwiches and one of the restaurant's popular milkshakes. Some customers, though, still prefer to come inside to what a wooden sign identifies as the "dinning room," which is located toward the rear of the building.

The barbecue here is actually pretty doggone good, despite the changeover in cooking method. Lacking the intense hickory flavor that characterizes the meat at the Chapel Hill restaurant, the chopped pork is, nevertheless, tender and moist. The sauce, which has no tomato paste, leaves a nice, peppery aftertaste and best complements the meat when it's sprinkled on a sandwich topped with coleslaw. (In fact the sauce may be practically the same sauce used by Keith Allen at his place.) The homemade, skins-on French fries are a tasty treat as well.

Frankly, the prices seem pretty steep, especially compared to those at other restaurants that use laborsaving gas or electric pits.

The Allen & Son name is a proud one in North Carolina barbecue circles, but the Bynum restaurant seems to be trading a bit on the reputation established here earlier by the genuine pit cooking of James Allen and continued more recently by Keith Allen in Chapel Hill. If you're in the neighborhood, though, it's definitely worth checking out.

CLYDE COOPER'S BARBECUE

109 East Davie Street
Raleigh, N.C. 27601
919-832-7614
Lunch and dinner (until 6:00 P.M.) Monday through Saturday

Clyde Cooper's Barbecue is a barbecue institution in downtown Raleigh.

The restaurant opened by the late Clyde Cooper near the corner of Davie and Wilmington Streets has been *the* place for barbecue in downtown Raleigh since 1938. Clyde Cooper's Barbecue has served a clientele made up largely of lawyers, judges, politicians, and businessmen. The eastern-style chopped pork isn't pit-cooked, and it would go totally unnoticed in a blind taste test. But barbecue in Raleigh—and much of the rest of the state, for that matter—has always been as much about ritual as about flavor. There's something almost sacramental about a visit to Cooper's two long, narrow rooms with the stamped tin ceilings and the antique "Rainbow Gasoline & Motor Oil" pump in the corner.

The food here is unadorned and straight from the heart of tobacco country: vinegar-splashed barbecue, Brunswick stew, slaw, boiled potatoes, hush puppies, and pork skins. It's what Raleigh

News & Observer columnist Dennis Rogers calls "the holy grub." Sure, you can also find ribs and barbecued chicken, along with some pretty good vegetables such as collard greens or corn and butterbeans, but the backbone of the business is the traditional barbecue plate or dinner.

Order your barbecue chopped, coarse ("coarse" is similar to "pulled"), or sliced. No matter which style you choose, it will be flavored with lots of salt, red pepper, and vinegar, but there will be absolutely no smoky taste.

Cooper's Brunswick stew has a good, robust taste and is suitably sweet for this region of the state. However, the stew has random green beans and stray pintos floating around in it—the owners should know better.

A barbecue plate includes both pork skins and hush puppies. The corn bread is smooth-textured and sweet, although not crispy enough for my tastes. On the other hand, the pork skins provide enough added crunch to make up for it.

The slaw contains no mayonnaise or mustard—just cabbage, vinegar, sugar, and a little minced carrot.

Cooper's iced tea is worth a refill or three, but don't bother with the desserts: they're store-bought and not worth the trouble.

Because of the number of "suits" who often fill the place, people in Raleigh refer to Cooper's fare as "power barbecue," but the place is still just a barbecue joint, after all, so whatever you want to wear will be just fine.

Don Murray's Barbecue & Seafood

2751 Capital Boulevard
Raleigh, N.C. 27604
919-872-6270
Lunch and dinner Monday through Saturday

Same ownership:
Barbecue Lodge
4600 Capital Boulevard
Raleigh, N.C. 27604
919-872-4755
Lunch and dinner Monday through Saturday

With its dollhouse-sized miniature of the restaurant sitting atop a brick pillar beside the street, Don Murray's Barbecue & Seafood on Capital Boulevard, just north of the U.S. 440 Beltline, is a familiar sight to Triangle residents. Murray owns not only this location but also the newer Barbecue Lodge further north on Capital Boulevard. Inside, Don Murray's has a pine-paneled main dining room and a huge, dividable side room. Aside from its newer, more modern décor, Barbecue Lodge is very, very similar to the older Don Murray location except that the newer facility doesn't have a buffet and offers a vegetable selection, which varies according to the day of the week. (Each day's selection is charted on the menu.) Both locations specialize in barbecue with all the trimmings, fried seafood, fried chicken, ribs, chicken & pastry, a wide selection of home-style vegetables, and cobblers and banana pudding.

The eastern-style barbecue served at both locations, which is *not* pit-cooked, is nevertheless quite good. For one thing, it has the spicy-hot, salty taste, which coastal-plain barbecue is supposed to have, but it doesn't overwhelm that taste with vinegar. Some people may find it a bit too peppery, but for me it's seasoned just about perfectly. The bottled sauce tastes like it contains vinegar, salt, red pepper flakes, and perhaps several dashes of hot sauce, but there's little evidence of ground red or black pepper or of sugar.

Along with the barbecue, I had soft, eastern-style boiled potatoes, which were, thankfully, not the canned variety; a so-so Brunswick stew containing superfluous green beans; and well-seasoned and well-cooked, but not overcooked, collard greens. The hush puppies were suitably light brown and crispy, but the tea was just a little too sweet for me—although an extra scoop of crushed ice would have cured that.

The buffet at Don Murray's is a country feast, with pork barbecue, fried and barbecued chicken, deep-fried pork chops, fried fish, beef stew and rice, all sorts of seasonal vegetables, and a couple of dessert choices. Murray's fried chicken, in particular, is very good, with a peppery, not-too-crispy crust that locks plenty of juice inside.

All in all, the food at these two restaurants is tasty, balanced, and predictable: comfort food without many peaks or valleys.

MURRAY'S BARBECUE & SEAFOOD
4700 Old Poole Road
Raleigh, N.C. 27610
919-237-6258
Lunch and dinner Monday through Friday

Located just a short distance from Raleigh's Interstate 440 Beltline, Murray's Barbecue & Seafood is a spot where the barbecue

Murray's Barbecue & Seafood cooks with wood on Raleigh's Old Poole Road, not far from the Interstate 440 Beltline.

is still cooked on wood-burning pits. Just about every day, you'll see the parking lot and the adjacent road shoulders jammed with the vehicles of a largely blue-collar crowd. What more could you possibly ask of a barbecue joint?

Not to be confused with *Don* Murray's on Capital Boulevard, Murray's Barbecue & Seafood has the perfect look. The unimpressive white cinder-block building sits beside a winding road lined with modest bungalows and mobile homes. Inside the restaurant, the smoking and non-smoking dining rooms are decorated with checked curtains and NASCAR photographs.

Generally speaking, local health departments don't take kindly to the sooty smoke stains and ashes produced by real, old-fashioned pit cooking. Their employees often seem zealously committed to making sure that all barbecue is eventually cooked in freshly scrubbed, stainless-steel boxes. But despite what the owner sees as frequent carping by the health department about the wood-burning pits, Murray's has managed to uphold the tradition of cooking with real wood. The customers show their support for Murray's stubborn adherence to the old custom by keeping the place hopping.

The barbecue at Murray's, which is not chopped too finely and has a distinct wood-smoke flavor, is served on paper plates in *very* generous portions. The eastern-style barbecue is salty, with a strong taste of vinegar, but it doesn't have too much pepper for the average palate. Buttered boiled potatoes, cooked with a hint of sugar, and eastern-style slaw are both on the same level as the barbecue. Although the hush puppies are tasty, they seem a little too uniform in shape not to have been purchased pre-made and frozen. Granted, nearly all restaurants use commercial hush puppy mixes that merely require the addition of water, but pups made from freshly mixed batter still taste just a touch better than the frozen ones to most people.

Murray's also features authentic Brunswick stew, fried and barbecued chicken, chicken wings, chicken & pastry, ribs (on Monday and Thursday), all kinds of fried seafood, and home-style vegetables (including tasty collards). A look around the crowded dining rooms shows that the customers are ordering and enjoying a bit of everything on the menu.

To get to Murray's, take the Poole Road Exit off the Interstate 440 Beltline, east of downtown Raleigh. You will then quickly bear right onto Old Poole Road and go 0.6 mile. Murray's is on the right.

OLE TIME BARBECUE

6309 Hillsborough Street
Raleigh, N.C. 27607
919-834-2511
Breakfast, lunch, and dinner Monday through Friday
Breakfast and lunch on Saturday

Ole Time Barbecue is a little place with middle-of-the-pack barbecue, but it has a lighthearted atmosphere and a friendly staff that makes you want to come back.

Located in a small cinder-block building not far from the state fairgrounds in Raleigh, Ole Time Barbecue is just about always packed with customers who obviously enjoy the restaurant's eastern-style barbecue, Brunswick stew, and other fixin's. The seating is a little close in the compact dining areas, and the noise level is usually pretty high, but the atmosphere is pleasant nonetheless. Wood paneling, red gingham curtains, assorted signs, miniature pigs, and bric-a-brac contribute to the overall impression of warmth and benign clutter.

This is not a log burner, so there's no smoke flavor to the meat here, but the pork is hand-chopped to an attractive chunky consistency, and it's tender. There are regular and hot eastern-style sauces, both said to be made from the recipe of the owner's grandfather, who lived in Snow Hill, and both are very good. The slaw atop your sandwich, or garnishing your barbecue plate, is creamy and a little sweeter than most. It contains both chopped carrots and what appears to be chopped bread-and-butter pickles. The hush puppies are tiny, crisp, and sweet, nicely balancing the rather mild barbecue.

Brunswick stew, ribs, and barbecued chicken are all on the menu at Ole Time, but I have to confess I've never tried them. The reason for this is that I always go to this place just to get a basic barbecue fix. As the menu points out, it's a nice place to go to simply get "porked."

RED, HOT & BLUE
6615 Falls of the Neuse Road
Raleigh, N.C. 27615
919-846-7427
Lunch and dinner daily at all locations

Other locations:

100 East Colonade Way
Cary, N.C. 27511
919-851-2782

115 Elliott Street
Chapel Hill, N.C. 27514
919-942-7427

2530 North Sardis Road
Charlotte, N.C. 28227
704-814-9940

445 Westwoods Shopping Center
Fayetteville, N.C. 28303
910-867-2810

Let's acknowledge right up front that Red, Hot & Blue is one of the cleverest names for a barbecue place in America. Let's also acknowledge that right under our noses, Red, Hot & Blue has come into North Carolina and attracted a big share of the market selling *Memphis*-style barbecue. What's worse, our state now has so many people who moved here from somewhere else that a great many aren't even aware that there is a difference between real, North Carolina barbecue and the pulled pork characteristic of the western Tennessee city. Add to all this the fact that Red, Hot & Blue barbecue is now what's sold at UNC home football games in Chapel Hill's Kenan stadium. Well, some will say that we have unquestionably strayed too far from our roots and that our shame is pretty well complete.

On the other hand, North Carolina has always been known for a certain tolerance that's sometimes missing from the states of the Deep South. Perhaps we should simply show hospitality to this interloper from the banks of the Mississippi and keep smiling bravely.

The barbecue served at Red, Hot & Blue is prepared on electric cookers, to which hickory chips or chunks are added to give the meat a smoky flavor. This method actually works pretty well and has the advantage of keeping the meat fairly moist. Much the same result is achieved by keeping charcoal or wood coals to one or both sides of the meat, thus surrounding the meat with pure smoke. By comparison, when North Carolina barbecue is cooked over wood coals, the glowing embers are spread directly underneath the meat. The dripping fat drops onto the coals and produces little spouts of fragrant steam in addition to the smoke swirling around the pit. Generally speaking, the indirect method described above or its imitator, the smoke-producing electric pit, is most often used to cook the barbecue produced in the states to the west of the Tar Heel state. On the other hand, the method used for most North Carolina barbecue delivers the best taste characteristics of both smoking and grilling. Having said all this, it is probably sufficient to all but the most discriminating barbecue aficionado that the meat cooked at Red, Hot & Blue has a satisfyingly smoky flavor.

Each of this Memphis-style barbecue chain's locations has an interior design built around a blues music theme. There are lots of framed flyers advertising blues shows and concerts, photos of well-known and not-so-well-known blues musicians, and even some real musical instruments hanging on the walls. There's lots of neon, including electric blue strings in a wall decoration consisting of twin pigs wearing shades and playing guitars.

The restaurant makes no bones about advertising "Memphis Pit Bar-b-que," which includes pig, chicken, and beef. They also offer sides of baked beans, potato salad, French fries, coleslaw, and collard greens. For our purposes, we're going to ignore the other meat offerings and concentrate on the pulled pork sandwich because, all of our condescension to the contrary, it actually compares very favorably with the better North Carolina-style barbecue sandwiches.

Heresy, you say? Well, consider that the pulled pork is really pretty similar to the coarse chopped barbecue found in many Lexington-style establishments. They both have plenty of chewy bits of outside-brown meat. The pulled pork sandwich is served on a plain bun. While the coleslaw adorning the sandwich is forgettable, the meat itself is tender, smoky, and flavorful. The unlabeled, vinegar-based sauce, bottled in a glass cruet seemingly as an afterthought, really isn't bad. You always have the option of bringing in your own sauce. Just take my advice and stay away from the "Mojo Mild," "Sufferin' Sweet," "Big Mama's" (mustard-based), and "Hoochie Coochie" (really, really hot) sauces, because . . . well, because these range about as far away from the North Carolina tradition as you can get, and because we simply have to draw the line somewhere.

SHORT SUGAR'S DRIVE-IN

1338 South Scales Street
Reidsville, N.C. 26992
336-342-7487
Curb service is offered

Second location:
2215 Riverside Drive
Danville, Va. 24540
804-793-4800
Both locations: Breakfast, lunch, and dinner Monday through Saturday

Here it is...the barbecue place with the greatest name in America! It seems that Johnny, Clyde, and Eldridge Overby had planned to open the Overby Brothers Drive-In. But two days before the scheduled opening in June 1949, Eldridge Overby, who was nicknamed "Short Sugar," was killed in an auto accident. Johnny and Clyde decided to honor their deceased brother by naming the business after him.

Short Sugar's looks like what it is: a place straight out of the 1950s. You can even still park in one of the old drive-in spaces and toot your horn for curb service. The barbecue brought out to the cars or served inside at this well-known spot was once cooked entirely over hardwood coals. Today, its pork hams and shoulders are started on an electric pit out back. After six hours they're moved to two small, wood-burning pits near the counter, where they cook for another four hours. To me, the meat is still tender and full of flavor, and the smoky taste doesn't seem diminished by the fact that the wood cooking took place late in the overall process.

People rave about the sauce at Short Sugar's, and many customers buy bottles to take home. Indeed, the restaurant's entire reputation seems to have been built largely on this thin, dark mixture. It has a definite overtone of Worcestershire and sugar but very little of the tomato that's often added to the vinegar base of Lexington-style dips.

One menu item at Short Sugar's that's an absolute mystery to me is *minced* barbecue. This is pork that's ground ultra-fine and served swimming in sauce, almost like barbecue chili. Why anyone would want to order it, rather than the regular chopped or sliced barbecue, is beyond me. One thing we can all agree on, though, is that, all in all, Short Sugar's is considered one of the top barbecue places in the Piedmont, if not the entire state.

BOB MELTON'S BARBECUE
501 Old Mill Road
Rocky Mount, N.C. 27803
252-446-8513
Lunch and dinner Monday through Saturday
Lunch only on Sunday

The original Bob Melton's Barbecue was probably North Carolina's first real, sit-down barbecue restaurant. The original location stood beside the Tar River in Rocky Mount for 75 years, before repeated floods forced a move to modern quarters at a high-and-dry site near U.S. 301.

Ironically, the riverbank location was under water when Bob Melton bought the land around 1921. Since all he originally planned to do was build a rough barbecue pit and sell pit-cooked barbecue to take home (along with making a little legal whiskey),

Many Tar Heels believe it just isn't barbecue if it isn't cooked over wood.

perhaps he didn't think floods would cause any great loss. However, he ended up opening a primitive restaurant on the site in 1924. This business was flooded, remodeled and expanded, then flooded again numerous times over the decades until the insurance company finally balked at paying for any more rebuilding after 1999's Hurricane Floyd.

Despite the flooding, Melton's became famous, and *Life* magazine crowned Melton the "king of southern barbecue" in 1958. Unfortunately, the real, wood-burning pits disappeared years ago, well before the move to the new location. Today the name and the basic menu are just about all that remain of this Tar Heel institution.

The original dishes—barbecue, slaw, Brunswick stew, and boiled potatoes—still anchor the menu, although nowadays the 'cue comes from gas-cooked pork shoulders, rather than wood-cooked whole hogs. It's seasoned in a straight eastern style, with plenty of salt, red pepper, and vinegar, no smoke flavor, and it's machine-chopped to a very fine consistency. The yellow slaw and crispy hush puppies are relatively unchanged over the years, but the Brunswick stew is basically an inauthentic canned product.

There's a fried chicken/barbecue combination plate, as well as a pork barbecue/barbecued chicken combo. Customers can also order from among 15 home-style vegetables. Daily specials include barbecued pork chops, pot roast and mashed potatoes, an unspecified "Blue Plate Special" each Wednesday, and "pig pickin'-style" pulled pork. Seafood platters and dinners are also available, along with the standard desserts.

Bob Melton's offers predictable, eastern-style comfort food, with nothing on the menu that's either outstanding or below an acceptable standard. There isn't a thing anyone can do about it, but now that Melton's is far removed from its former shady, riverside site, this restaurant just doesn't offer the same experience that it once did.

GARDNER'S BARBECUE 'N' CHICKEN
1331 North Wesleyan Boulevard
Rocky Mount, N.C. 27804
252-446-2983
Lunch and dinner daily

The menu here says, "Gardner's Barbecue Voted North Carolina's Best," without specifying when or where this referendum occurred. While there would undoubtedly be disagreement over whether the place deserves quite *that* high an honor, most people would probably go along with a claim that stated, "Gardner's

Barbecue Voted Pretty Decent."

Gardner's actually does have tasty barbecue, considering that there's no hint of the meat having been anywhere near wood coals. I did overhear several customers remarking on how much they liked the restaurant's typical eastern-style sauce. For those watching their cholesterol, there's also chopped turkey barbecue, which is very finely chopped and drier than the pork barbecue, due to the lower fat content.

The crisp-skinned, flavorful fried chicken at Gardner's is a real treat, but the oven-cooked chicken in barbecue sauce is a little less noteworthy. If chicken is among your favorites, you can also order entrées of fried chicken livers or gizzards. There's pretty good chicken and pastry, as well, although the latter doesn't quite have the rich, full flavor I've encountered elsewhere.

In my opinion, Gardner's Brunswick stew isn't really representative of the best the Rocky Mount region has to offer. It contains a spice I couldn't identify or recognize as typical. The vegetables on the lunch buffet were mostly middling, except for some truly outstanding collards on the day I visited. I generally felt the same way about the desserts, with the exception of the sweet-potato fried pies called "potato jacks," which were very good.

The sweet tea is too sweet by half, but then you always have the option of ordering "half-and-half," which I overheard several customers doing.

You won't feel like you've been to barbecue Mecca after a visit to Gardner's, but you'll certainly leave well fed.

Richard's Barbecue

522 North Main Street
Salisbury, N.C. 28144
704-636-9563
Breakfast, lunch, and dinner Monday through Saturday

Richard's Barbecue is a cozy place, which has been in business since 1979, on downtown Salisbury's North Main Street. Its gray-brick exterior with red awnings and its inviting interior are kept as neat as a pin. The main room, which is accented by toy trains, has an unusually long, stainless steel counter. Back behind the restaurant, where the pit and the woodpile are located, the parking lot routinely stays full. It's obvious that Richard's is a popular local gathering place, since there are usually people waiting for available booths, tables, and counter stools.

Presiding over this enterprise is Richard Monroe, who learned his craft working for Salisbury's famed T&F Barbecue. T&F opened for business in 1935 and for quite some time was known as "the biggest little place in North Carolina." Remember, Salisbury is very proud of its barbecue heritage. Some accounts say Salisbury's barbecue history even pre-dates Lexington's.

The barbecue here is closely akin to Lexington-style barbecue, but it has its own Rowan County vinegar tang. The pit-cooked pork shoulders are served chopped and sliced. Both have a very lean consistency and a pronounced and pleasant smoky taste. Barbecue slaw here is slightly less sweet than what's usually found in Lexington. To round out your barbecue meal, there are enormous hush puppies, nearly the size of tennis balls.

Richard's also has a complete breakfast menu. Like all traditional places in this area, the breakfast selections include that wonderful specialty brought to the area by settlers of German ancestry—

livermush. This romantic-sounding stuff is a mixture of ground pork liver, cornmeal, and seasonings. Throughout a large swath of the Piedmont, livermush is served sliced and fried, either as a breakfast meat or in sandwiches.

Richard's also has barbecued chicken, a salad bar, and a wide sandwich selection. Dinner specials include homemade chili beans and homemade spaghetti, both of which are available after 4:00 P.M.

You can easily find your way to Richard's by following East Innes Street (U.S. 52) from Interstate 85 toward downtown. When you reach downtown, turn right on to North Main. The restaurant is several blocks down on the left.

WINK'S KING OF BARBECUE
509 Faith Road
Salisbury, N.C. 28146
704-637-2410
Breakfast, lunch, and dinner Monday through Saturday

For many years, Wink's occupied a modest, red-painted building on U.S. 52, just east of its intersection with Interstate 85. People used to comment that while the building wasn't much to look at, "the hickory smoke would grab your nose a half-mile away."

Now, the old building has been torn down because of roadwork in the area, and Wink's has moved to a new location not far from its original spot.

I was gratified to see the wood-burning pit and the pile of quartered logs at the fancy new facility. Hopefully the aromatic smoke from the pit will drift back over the spot where Wink's used to stand, reminding everyone that the business is still cooking barbecue the old-fashioned way, just a short distance up the road.

The new building that houses Wink's King of Barbecue couldn't be more different from the original. Instead of one dark, low-ceilinged room, there are now two large dining rooms, with lots of light-colored, diagonal wood paneling and other modern decorating touches in evidence.

At the average barbecue joint, radical changes like these in the physical environment can cause serious apprehension about how the barbecue itself may have changed ("This place is nice...*too nice*."), but I'm happy to report that the 'cue at Wink's is still very, very good. It's smoky, sweet, tender, and, atypical for this region, served with white slaw, rather than the red barbecue variety.

Since the new digs are really a touch too elegant for barbecue alone, it's appropriate that you can get just about anything you want at Wink's. The breakfast menu is expansive, including that Piedmont crescent favorite—livermush. You can also choose from a menu that includes seafood, steak, prime rib, salads, stuffed baked potatoes, and a wide sandwich selection. There's a prime-rib sandwich and another sandwich featuring homemade pimento cheese on a croissant.

The new Wink's is easy to find. From Interstate 85, take the exit for U.S. 52 East, going toward Albemarle. Go about a half-mile and bear right on Faith Road. The restaurant is a short distance on the right.

GREEN RIVER BAR-B-QUE

131 Main Street
Saluda, N.C. 28773
828-749-9892
Lunch and dinner Monday through Saturday
Lunch until 3:00 P.M. on Sunday

Since 1984, the mountain community of Saluda, located near the South Carolina border, has been home to Green River Bar-B-Que. During that time Green River has developed an ambiance that defies easy characterization. Kim and Melanie Talbot, a couple who moved to the North Carolina mountains from coastal South Carolina, turn out really good barbecue. They also keep things interesting with unusual side dishes and desserts that are a step up from normal barbecue-restaurant fare.

After crossing a covered porch, which shelters a couple of picnic tables, you enter a small, cheerful dining room. The room contains a dozen or so round wooden tables with ladder-back chairs, most of them occupied. A bench beside the door is also steadily occupied by a parade of local residents showing up to claim takeout orders.

I had noticed from the parking lot that the pit area and the woodpile looked quite unused, so I was intrigued to read on the menu that the barbecue at Green River is "smoked over hickory and green oak." A framed old newspaper clipping on the wall refers to Green River's pit cooking. I discovered that the folks at Green River started out cooking over real wood coals, but that they switched fairly recently to electric cookers. These cookers are equipped with boxes in which wood chips or chunks smolder and produce fairly heavy smoke.

Whatever they do, it definitely works for me. I was served a plate absolutely chock-full of food. The plate was anchored by a generous serving of finely chopped, very lean barbecue, sprinkled through with bits of the chewy outside-brown layer. The meat was as tender, juicy, and smoky as anyone could expect. Although it really didn't need any sauce at all, I noticed that there were bottles containing three separate varieties of sauce on each table. The first was a mild, Lexington-style dip, perhaps a little thicker than normal. The second had a similar consistency but packed some real heat. The third, a mustard-based concoction, was evidence of the owners' South Carolina roots.

Tasty versions of both white and barbecue coleslaw were available, along with large, dark brown "shaggy dog" hush puppies with a coarse, grainy exterior. But one of the things I most enjoyed was a half 'n' half order of homemade French fries and sweet-potato fries. The well-cooked sweet-potato fries were both salty and sweet and had a crispy exterior. These fries went very well with the savory pork and offered a great change of pace. I couldn't help wondering why more places don't serve sweet-potato fries.

Other unusual side dishes included fried-green tomatoes, baked-potato salad, creamed spinach, and tomato pie.

The servings were so large that I had absolutely no room left for dessert. However, I did notice a wall-mounted menu advertising something called "chocolate suicide cake," along with mixed-berry and apple cobbler and homemade sweet-potato pie. I gathered that delicious desserts are a real point of pride for the Talbots, so I'm just going to have to find my way back soon.

Saluda is located on U.S. 176, midway between Hendersonville and Tryon. Take Exit 28 from Interstate 26, then turn right onto U.S. 176 (Main Street). Look for the restaurant on the left, just after you pass the tiny, picturesque downtown block.

ALSTON BRIDGES BARBECUE

620 East Grover Street
Shelby, N.C. 28150
704-482-1998
Lunch and dinner Tuesday through Saturday

This third-generation, family-owned restaurant is the second of two in Shelby founded by men who learned all about how to pit-cook Lexington-style barbecue from Warner Stamey, the Piedmont barbecue pioneer. In this case, Stamey taught his secrets to his brother-in-law, Alston Bridges, who is no relation to Stamey's other Shelby apprentice, Red Bridges. Alston's son and three of his grandchildren now run Alston Bridges Barbecue.

Even though the pork shoulders are started out here on electric cookers, they're still cooked long and slow over real wood coals. The tenderness and delightful wood-smoked flavor of the meat indicates that the method is working extraordinarily well. In fact, tenderness is such a big factor among the members of the Bridges family that a special fork is used to test the shoulders for doneness. Although "the fork" has been lost or broken several times, it has always been recovered and is currently in good repair.

Perhaps because Shelby is so far west, the definition of barbecue is stretched a little bit here to include not only pork ribs, which are pit-cooked in almost exactly the same way as the Lexington-style shoulders, but also beef ribs and beef brisket. The ribs and other dishes are a delicious, tender, perfectly turned-out change of pace. However, make no mistake: the pit-cooked pork is still squarely in the mainstream of the Lexington tradition. Some customers may find the everyday chopped barbecue a little fine for their tastes, but Bridges will be glad to accommodate requests for a chunkier texture. At least one couple I encountered had just driven from

Morganton to Shelby for some of Alston Bridges' barbecue and peppery-vinegar sauce. By some definitions, that makes this "50-mile barbecue."

I suggest you step outside the traditional range of side dishes to try some of Alston Bridges' extraordinary baked beans. Cooked with onion, bacon, bell pepper, and brown sugar, they set off the smoky flavor of the barbecue to absolute perfection.

To find Alston Bridges Barbecue, take the U.S. 74 Bypass west. Opposite Shelby High School, turn north onto DeKalb Street. Follow DeKalb until it dead-ends opposite the hospital. Turn right onto Grover Street. You'll see the restaurant a block-and-a-half down on the right.

BRIDGES BARBECUE LODGE
2000 East Dixon Boulevard (U.S. 74 Bypass)
Shelby, N.C. 28152
704-482-8567
Lunch and dinner (or until the barbecue runs out) Wednesday through Sunday
Closed Monday and Tuesday

Bridges Barbecue Lodge has the distinction of being one of two places in Shelby whose founders learned all the finer points of Lexington-style barbecue directly under the supervision of the legendary Warner Stamey.

What Red Bridges learned from Stamey in the 1930s he began putting into practice for himself in 1946, when he started Bridges Barbecue Lodge. Ever since Red's death in the mid-1960s, his wife

Lyttle (pronounced *Light-ul*) has been the heart and soul of the place, not only carrying on Red's legacy but stamping her own work ethic and personality on the restaurant. Around Bridges, she's known as Mama B. or "the redhead," and she's built a reputation for cleanliness and order that's totally out of character with most people's conception of what a barbecue joint is supposed to be. She proudly says she has "the cleanest floors in the barbecue business," and her neatly stacked and aligned woodpile looks as though it's been dusted.

Mama B. and her daughter Debbie, an attractive former model, like to keep things uncomplicated around the place. There's no menu, just a brief listing of items on the little pads the waitresses use to take orders. Everything is focused on cooking and serving the most tender, moist, smoke-flavored, perfectly textured barbecue that it's possible to produce. The barbecue is served on a plain bun with red barbecue slaw or in a tray with some slaw and hush puppies on the side. If you're in Bridges Barbecue Lodge for anything else, except possibly to josh with Debbie and Mama B. from your place at one of the counter stools up front, you're basically wasting your time.

Everything more or less pales in comparison to the heavenly, smoke-tinged meat here, although the loose-crusted, brown hush puppies, which I call "shaggy dogs," seem to hold their crispness longer than most. The tart red coleslaw puts a deliciously hard, tangy edge on the mild sweetness of the barbecued pork. You'll also like the green ceramic teapots brought to each table for iced-tea refills and the fact that Bridges' thick, mild dip is served hot in a little container on the side.

Be aware of the fact that Bridges Barbecue Lodge closes for one week each July and during the week after Christmas. According to Debbie, this happens so Mama B. can lift up everything in the place and clean under it—and maybe dust that woodpile while no one's watching.

WHITE SWAN BARBECUE

3198 U.S. 301 South
Smithfield, N.C. 27577
919-934-8913
Lunch and dinner daily

Other locations:

U.S. 70 East
Pine Level, N.C. 27568
919-202-5932

U.S. 70 East Bypass
Wilsons Mills, N.C. 27593
919-989-6500

U.S. 70 East
Clayton, N.C. 27520
919-550-2551

Interstate 40 and N.C. 210 (Exit 319)
McGee's Crossroads
Willow Spring, N.C. 27592
919-989-9299

The original White Swan is an absolutely delightful little place, with great food and a personable, fun-loving owner, Linwood Parker, who has spun off from this first location to form a small, area barbecue chain.

The restaurant is only a two-room affair. On one side, there is a utilitarian space containing a kitchen, takeout counter, and two or three tables. On the other is a charming little dining room, which seats 30. It has varnished wood walls and ceiling and curved, wood-slat benches.

Barbecue was cooked over real hardwood coals at White Swan for 41 years, but Parker switched to electric pits after he bought the place in 1988. He's a great storyteller and something of a politician, so he tells everyone with a perfectly straight face that he had to change because some of his customers "were complaining about the wood-smoke taste." The amazing thing is that everyone buys his story. In fact, the barbecue is cooked so moist and tender at White Swan, and the rest of the menu is so great, that little seems to have been lost.

The chopped pork, which is somewhat of an eastern anomaly, since it's prepared from shoulders rather than whole hogs, has an appetizing, mild seasoning and lots of crunchy brown-outside bits. A crisp brown piece of fried pork skin garnishes every barbecue plate. The slaw is white and creamy, and the hush puppies are some of the best you'll ever eat. The corn bread is light as a feather and cooked to a perfect golden-brown in fresh oil, which is heated to exactly 350 degrees.

Try to plan your visit so you'll be hungry enough to try some of the White Swan's legendary fried chicken along with your barbecue plate. And try not to be in a rush, because if you're fortunate, the gregarious Linwood Parker will be on hand, visiting with every customer and making everyone feel very much at home.

To get to the original White Swan, take Exit 90 off Interstate 95 and go toward Smithfield on U.S. 301/N.C. 96 North. The restaurant is 1½ miles on the left.

Speedy Lohr's Barbecue

10774 N.C. 8 South
Southmont, N.C. 27351
336-798-1538
Breakfast, lunch, and dinner daily

Speedy Lohr learned his craft while working with the late Warner Stamey, a giant among North Carolina pit masters. He is also a former owner of Speedy's Barbecue in Lexington, which kept that name after Speedy Lohr sold it. For quite a few years since then, Speedy and his wife have operated Speedy Lohr's Barbecue, an unpretentious, laid-back café located in the waterside community of Southmont at High Rock Lake, some 8 miles from Interstate 85.

The Southmont restaurant's building doesn't look like much from the outside, and the interior is a bit dark and cramped, but there are brick chimneys and a real pile of wood slabs outside. That's all anyone really needs to know to give any barbecue place at least preliminary approval.

The first thing anyone will notice is that Speedy Lohr's serves a very generous portion of chopped barbecue on a sandwich. But the second thing is that here, in the heart of the Piedmont, this restaurant serves a barbecue sandwich that almost any easterner would enjoy and claim as his own. Rather than the typical sweet-and-sour Lexington dip, Speedy Lohr's developed a sauce recipe that's mostly vinegar, salt, and pepper, with very little tomato ketchup and not much sugar or other sweetener. The meat itself is moderately smoky and lean, with a nice chunky texture. Topped with Speedy's peppery barbecue slaw, it makes a delicious sandwich that sort of combines the best features of both eastern- and Lexington-style barbecue.

Barbecued chicken, cooked over wood coals, is on the menu on Friday, Saturday, and Sunday.

Speedy Lohr's has all the usual offerings for breakfast, as well as quite a few sandwich choices, including his trademark Big Cheeseburger, a good-looking hamburger-steak sandwich, and, of course, sandwiches made from the area's famous Conrad & Hinkle pimento cheese, which is mixed up in a tiny, old-fashioned grocery store in downtown Lexington. Speedy Lohr's makes its own homemade spaghetti sauce and offers a tempting and reasonably priced ribeye steak basket (not a sandwich) with French fries.

Speedy Lohr's is all about taste, rather than atmosphere, but the taste is so good that the drive to Southmont is worthwhile.

CAROLINA BAR-B-Q
213 Salisbury Road
Statesville, N.C. 28677
704-873-5585
Lunch and dinner Monday through Saturday

The distinguishing visual characteristic at Carolina Bar-B-Q is the restaurant name displayed in large white letters, along with a sizeable pig cutout, on the steeply pitched, Carolina-blue roof. Glancing around at a full parking lot, you'll also notice the brick pit chimney and a good-sized woodpile, all of which are very encouraging signs.

You won't be disappointed. The late Charles Kuralt mentioned this place in his book *Charles Kuralt's America*, although the reference

Carolina Bar-B-Q in Statesville uses hardwood coals.

was actually tongue-in-cheek criticism that the barbecue didn't have the amount of fat and skin Kuralt was used to in barbecue joints Down East. Indeed, owner Gene Medlin proudly told me, "We remove all the fat and gristle." In fact, I did find the chopped pork was as "lean 'n' clean" as anyone could ask for, and maybe even more than some folks prefer.

The barbecue served here is actually closer to eastern North Carolina whole-hog barbecue than it is to the Lexington- or Piedmont-style you'd expect in this part of the state. It is fairly finely chopped and served with a faint vinegar flavor. You can choose from two very different sauces: a hot version, which has a definite vinegar-and-pepper attitude usually found in the east and a mild sauce, which is thick and red, with overtones of liquid smoke. I'd stick with the hot. The smoky flavor of the barbecue, though, is real, and I couldn't help pondering how much both regional styles of barbecue are improved by cooking over real wood coals. Everything—the slaw, the barbecue, and the huge round hush puppies—goes together very harmoniously.

I also sampled the tender barbecued chicken, which had a good, smoky taste, but it came with a fairly generic, thick sauce.

Gene Medlin is proud of Carolina Bar-B-Q's fresh-baked fruit cobblers. I had a serving of blackberry, which Gene insisted I top with ice cream. While I was much too full to finish it all, it was terrific. The iced tea is worth mentioning as well, since it's flavorful, not too sweet, and garnished with two lemon slices, just the way I like it best.

One item I didn't sample, although I wanted to, was what's billed on the menu as the "world's best foot-long hot dog."

Medlin does a lot of catering in the Statesville area, which no doubt helps stimulate trade at the restaurant. However, I have a feeling that even without the extra exposure the catering brings, the clean, attractive surroundings and the quality food at Carolina Bar-B-Q would still pack in the customers.

ANDY'S BARBECUE
6043 Old U.S. 52
Welcome, N.C. 27374
336-731-8207
Lunch and dinner Monday through Saturday
Curb Service

Andy's Barbecue is located in the peaceful village of Welcome, some six miles north of Lexington and ten miles south of Winston-Salem. It occupies a corner storefront in a small strip of buildings that includes a country store. It's a simple place—just a counter up front with Formica-topped tables filling a narrow, but fairly deep, dining room. But the elements that matter the most—the brick pit and large woodpile—are outside. Everyone driving Old U.S. 52, which is the main drag coming into Welcome, can plainly see them.

Andy's definitely has a 1950s feel about it. Curb service, from speedy waitresses who take and deliver orders at a trot, is available in the gravel parking lot adjoining the building. The parking lot is also where Andy's occasionally hosts live bands on Saturday nights. It isn't too hard to imagine some of the young, local "racin' " fans, and there are a *lot* of them in the neighborhood, gunning their engines and doing a few doughnuts in the loose gravel. This would all happen after hours, of course.

Although perhaps operated on a smaller scale than some others, this is an authentic, Lexington-style barbecue joint. Pork shoulders are roasted slowly over wood coals. The result is extremely tender, mild barbecue with a definite smoky flavor. The sandwiches are piled high with meat, and red barbecue slaw is added automatically unless you request otherwise.

Andy's has other sandwiches, tasty hot dogs, and a few plates that feature ham, steak, barbecued chicken, and chuck-wagon steak. Despite these offerings, the barbecue is still the main attraction.

KERLEY'S BARBECUE

5114 Old U.S. 52
Welcome, N.C. 27374
336-731-8245
Breakfast, lunch, and dinner Monday through Saturday

It's difficult to imagine that a town the size of Welcome can support one barbecue restaurant, much less two, but both Kerley's and Andy's (mentioned earlier) have been in business quite a while. For its first thirteen years, Kerley's was located in a smaller location that was also on Old U.S. 52. The large brick building that currently houses the restaurant was built in 1991.

Along with Lexington to the south and Winston-Salem to the north, Welcome is right smack dab in the middle of NASCAR country, and the interest in racing is evident at Kerley's. For one thing, the waitresses wear shirts imprinted with the Richard Childress team name and logo. (The Childress racing shop and museum are nearby.) Then too, one of the two dining rooms is completely decorated with framed NASCAR posters. Prints of rural scenes painted by Dempsey Essick, a local artist who has a gallery in Welcome, hang on the walls of the other dining room.

Although there's a brick pit and a woodpile outside Kerley's, my sliced barbecue sandwich, while certainly tasty, had little smoke flavor. It contained a slice of very white meat, obviously from the ham, which is unusual in an area that's best known for serving the slightly darker meat from pork shoulders. The sandwich was dressed with a very mild, well-balanced Lexington-style dip.

Kerley's serves plenty of specials, including pork chops, meat loaf, and country-style steak. They also occasionally even have baby-back ribs on special. All available dishes can be complemented with plenty of seasonal vegetables, cooked the old-fashioned way. You can even choose from a large breakfast selection, which is available every day except Sunday, when Kerley's is closed.

RALPH'S BARBECUE
1400 Julian R. Allsbrook Highway (U.S. 158)
Weldon, N.C. 27890
252-536-2101
Lunch and dinner daily

Many years after its founding in 1941, Ralph's Barbecue was located on a side street in Roanoke Rapids. Now it sits in the middle of a one-acre parking lot on U.S. 158, between Roanoke Rapids and Weldon. The large barn-roofed building is just the right size to accommodate the crowds of local patrons and travelers on Interstate 95. It's gussied up nicely with a green-canopied entrance and a row of pink neon pigs.

Patrons come to enjoy the expansive barbecue and country-cookin' buffet, order off the menu, or visit the busy takeout section. With its carpeting and gray-and-green interior color scheme, Ralph's looks a great deal more like a Holiday Inn restaurant than a barbecue joint, but the food is good, and the choices are interesting.

The menu consists basically of barbecue, which is served with Brunswick stew, slaw, and hush puppies, and sandwiches. The takeout counter offers sandwiches, barbecue and fixin's, seafood, fried and herb-roasted chicken, vegetables, and desserts. The buffet, which is priced at $ 5.95 for lunch Monday through Friday and $7.50 at all other times, is always available and understandably popular.

Ralph's doesn't really serve chopped barbecue. The pork here is either minced or "pulled," which the proprietors call "sliced." The minced barbecue is one step beyond chopped, much too fine for my personal taste, as well as being a little overloaded with vinegar and not quite salty enough. The so-called "sliced" barbecue is actually pulled apart in hunks, as it would be at a pig picking. If a whole pig is properly cooked, the meat easily falls into pieces with the touch of a hand, so there's no need to bring a sharp knife into the process.

The chunks of pork are tender and moist at Ralph's, and I recommend them rather than the minced-to-mush alternative. The sauce here is all vinegar, salt, and peppers, with little evidence of sugar.

I was gratified to find that the Brunswick stew on the buffet was delicious, with a great balance between sweet and savory. Much of the Brunswick stew cooked in the eastern third of the state is fairly sweet, unlike the Piedmont version. Eastern cooks either include or leave out cubed potatoes, according to their own wishes. This version had no potatoes.

Elsewhere on the buffet, I found fried and oven-roasted "barbecued" chicken; oven-roasted ribs in barbecue sauce; a wide variety of vegetables, including cabbage, tiny field peas, and collards (in season); and desserts. I tried a serving of very acceptable banana pudding with meringue topping and cherry cobbler with a sort of puff-pastry crust, which had gotten a little tough after being on the steam table for a while.

There's no wood-burning pit at Ralph's, but the place is highly regarded by local residents. I predict you'll enjoy the barbecue, particularly if you stick with the "pig picking" hunks of tender pork.

SHAW'S BAR-B-Q HOUSE

U.S. 64 Bypass
Williamston, N.C. 27892
252-792-5339
Breakfast, lunch, and dinner Monday through Saturday

Despite the misleading appearance of the false front on the building, Shaw's Bar-B-Q House is a compact place with only a half-dozen tables and nine or ten booths. Along with barbecue and some daily specials, it also sells fresh products from a glass-front meat case: freshly made sausage, sliced barbecue, and fresh pork tenderloin were on display when I visited. What was not on display was any evidence of a pit nor any signs of a woodpile, but then this is eastern North Carolina, which is largely gas-and-electricity country when it comes to barbecue.

I had a "pig and stew plate," which consisted of big hunks of pulled or pig-picking-style pork, stew, slaw, and potatoes. Shaw's also has chopped and sliced barbecue on plates and in sandwiches.

The pork was tender, but rather bland, even after the addition of the house sauce. There are actually two sauces: a subdued vinegar-and-pepper mixture and a "sweet" sauce, which is buttery and smooth. Shaw's sells the sauces for $8.50 per gallon.

Along with the barbecue, I had stewed, rather than boiled, potatoes, which were smooth and very good, with a nice, onion flavor. The yellow coleslaw was the finely chopped, mustard-based type, characteristic of this region. I found the Brunswick stew hearty, thick, and appealing, although not as sweet as most Brunswick stew served in the northeast quarter of the state. It also contained green peas, which is practically unheard-of in the region.

Homemade chicken & pastry is on special here on Monday and

Tuesday. There's barbecued chicken all the time, and there's a daily fish special.

Bread pudding, containing lots of raisins, provides an unusual and appetizing choice for dessert.

The very best barbecue in the Williamston area is found at backyard pig pickings, which are frequent and numerous. Shaw's provides the pork fixes in between.

STEPHENSON'S BARBECUE
12020 N.C. 50 North
Willow Spring, N.C. 27592
919-894-4530
Lunch and dinner Monday through Saturday

Despite a relatively out-of-the-way location, it's obvious that a lot of people have found their way to Stephenson's Barbecue. It's also obvious that they've spread the word, because the parking lot is nearly always full, and the attractive, natural wood-sided restaurant is crowded on most days.

Red-checked tablecloths and a picture window overlook a lovely landscaped area. This environment plus Stephenson's custom of serving food on real crockery plates, rather than paper or plastic, creates a very inviting atmosphere.

A worn-out, deeply hollowed wood chopping block in the entranceway bears witness to the hundreds of tons of barbecue that have been chopped at Stephenson's since Paul Stephenson founded the place in the early 1960s. Stephenson's son Andy (who helped wear away that chopping block as a youngster), Andy's wife Lynn, and Andy's daughter Amber are all directly involved in the business. Paul Stephenson's other son, Wayne, runs the family's nursery business adjacent to the restaurant. "Mr. Paul" is still around on most days, visiting from table to table with patrons and old friends. His wife Ann occasionally accompanies him.

Stephenson's cooks its pork-shoulder barbecue over hardwood charcoal, so the meat comes off the pits with a deep smoky flavor. But this is, after all, eastern North Carolina, and even though the barbecue doesn't come from whole hogs, it *is* seasoned with a typical blend of salt, peppers, vinegar, and other spices. The normal custom here is to chop the "beautiful meat" from the shoulders fairly coarsely, while the crusty brown-outside layer, crispy bits of skin, and a tiny amount of fat are chopped super fine and added to the mixture for texture and flavor. Coleslaw, barbecue potatoes, and hush puppies with a touch of onion fill out a barbecue plate.

On Thursdays, Stephenson's serves what has to be some of the best chicken & pastry found anywhere. Stewing hens are cooked in a large pot, and the boned, shredded meat is added back into the rich golden broth and layered with strips of hand-rolled pastry.

Slow-cooked and tender barbecued chicken and barbecued pork ribs, which are served on Thursday, Friday, and Saturday only, are favorites at Stephenson's. You can also find a variety of delicious country vegetables.

To get to Stephenson's take Interstate 40 to Exit 319 (McGee's Crossroads). This exit is midway between Raleigh and the intersection of Interstates 40 & 95. Drive west on N.C. 210 to its intersection with N.C. 50. Turn north on N.C. 50 and watch for Stephenson's on the right side, immediately past the nursery.

JACKSON'S BIG OAK BARBECUE

920 South Kerr Avenue
Wilmington, N.C. 28403
910-799-1581
Lunch and dinner Monday through Saturday

The motto at Jackson's Big Oak Barbecue is, "We ain't fancy, but we sure are good." In truth, Jackson's is the best place to go in Wilmington for a comforting dose of eastern-style barbecue.

The "Big Oak" in the restaurant's name refers to a landmark tree on the property, not to the presence of a woodpile. Jackson's approaches barbecue much like most other places in the coastal plain, in that the right combination of vinegar, salt, peppers, and spices, rather than wood-smoked flavor, is considered its defining characteristic.

Actually, a tacitly accepted system of romantic self-delusion about pit cooking has emerged in the region. A July 2001 editorial in the *Wilmington Star*, for example, described eastern barbecue thusly: "It is to be caressed for seven or eight hours in the aromatic warmth of smoldering hickory." The writer made these remarks undoubtedly knowing full well that there isn't a restaurant anywhere *near* Wilmington that cooks barbecue in that fashion.

In carefully chosen words, Jackson's says its barbecue "is slowly cooked and hickory smoked every night." This means that it's cooked in electric pits, with bits of wood added to produce smoke. What the heck! In a corner of the state where vinegar seems to be the be-all and end-all, let's give them credit for even *trying* to infuse the meat with a little smoke. The end product is tender and well seasoned, with crispy brown bits mixed with the lean meat for flavor.

Jackson's is a cheerful, busy place, with wood paneling and

pictures of local football players and other sports notables on the walls. The menu features the barbecue basics—chopped pork, slaw, barbecued chicken, ribs, Brunswick stew, eastern-style barbecued potatoes, hush puppies, and corn sticks. There is a nice selection of home-style vegetables, including country fries, baked beans, potato salad, candied yams, green beans, black-eyed peas, fried okra and, best of all, collards.

This may not exactly be a premier barbecue destination, but it's a good little place to stop when you're in the neighborhood, which is not far from UNC-Wilmington.

BILL'S BARBECUE AND CHICKEN
3007 Downing Street
Wilson, N.C. 27893
252-237-4372
Lunch and dinner Tuesday through Sunday

Bill Ellis is the biggest barbecue caterer in North Carolina, and he prides himself on the fact that his eighteen-wheelers, emblazoned with his name over a red silhouette of North Carolina, can do catering coast-to-coast, for customers from "one to a million." Actually, the coast-to-coast catering thing is more of a marketing gimmick than anything, although the company has gone as far as California to do a job.

But even Ellis's big name couldn't save his popular restaurant in Wilson from the floodwaters of Hurricane Floyd in September 1999. Undaunted, Ellis closed the damaged eatery and turned his attention to building a complex on the same property. Bill's

Barbecue and Chicken now has one building for a buffet, another for takeout and drive-through, and a third to house his own convention center.

The enormous dining room that houses Bill's buffet resembles a military mess hall, complete with gray walls and tables and a sign saying, "Take all you want, but eat all you take."

However, the buffet has far better food than any chow hall. It features barbecue; Brunswick stew; baked, fried, and barbecued chicken; a wide variety of vegetables; Salisbury steak; hot dogs; homemade sausage; fried fish; corn sticks, biscuits, and hush puppies; and desserts. Waiting in line to dig into all this, you can't help noticing the happy looks on the departing customers' faces. That look is, without question, one of the most welcome sights known to mankind.

Bill's buffet takes a novel approach to serving barbecue, paying tribute to the eastern North Carolina whole-hog tradition at the same time, by featuring a whole cooked pig laid out on a brick mock-up of a real pit. Of course, there's plenty of chopped barbecue already prepared and seasoned, along with the pulled and finger-shredded hunks of meat that are characteristic of the meat served at pig pickings.

Bill Ellis owns his own hog farms, where special feed helps produce some of the tenderest meat available. (He also has a small army of workers who give each pig a daily, 30-minute treatment with a hand-held electric massage unit—just kidding.) It's no surprise, then, that the shredded, pig-picking barbecue is delicious, especially when spiced up with a ladle full of Bill's sauce. The sauce comes from a stainless-steel container that has a layer of crushed red pepper flakes floating on top.

Boiled potatoes, cooked down in red pepper-flavored tomato stock, and collard greens (the yellowish "cabbage" variety) both get extremely high marks. The traditional yellow slaw provides an excellent contrast to the piquancy of the barbecue.

Here in the heart of eastern stew country, Bill's offers a dark, spicy Brunswick stew that's decidedly different. It contains yams, black-eyed peas, and green beans. It resembles spicy vegetable soup more than the thick, orange-colored stew that most people expect. While it takes some getting used to, it's quite appetizing.

If you finish all this off with a few glasses of superb iced tea and a serving of Bill's meringue-topped banana pudding, you'll leave with a smile on your face, too.

MITCHELL'S BARBECUE, RIBS & CHICKEN
606 Ward Boulevard S.E.
Wilson, N.C. 27893
252-291-9189
Lunch and dinner daily

This unusual restaurant started in a modest grocery store, which was operated for years by Ed Mitchell's parents in a predominantly black section of Wilson. One day not long after his father's death, Mitchell, who was already grown, came home for a visit and pit-cooked some barbecue to cheer up his mother, who was depressed over dwindling business. While he and his mother were eating in the back room, customers walked into the store, noticed the barbecue, and bought some to take home. With the glimmerings of an idea forming in his mind, Mitchell scrambled to cook more barbecue to sell the following day. Before long, word had spread, and Mitchell brought other family members on board to staff the new and promising venture.

The store was eventually turned into a cafeteria-style restaurant.

Tending the pit at Mitchell's Barbecue, Ribs & Chicken

It was located in a two-story cinder-block building with the restaurant name somewhat inexpertly painted on the outside in big green letters. The legend, "Cooked the old-fashioned way over charcoal" was similarly emblazoned on the exterior wall of the adjacent pit house. Both white and black customers turned off U.S. 301, found space in the tiny parking lot, and ventured past the colorful exterior to discover some of the best barbecue and soul food they had ever experienced. They found whole-hog barbecue cooked over live coals; ribs; fried and barbecued chicken; pork chops; down-home vegetables; and incredible desserts. Today, Mitchell's barbecue is still smoky, tongue-caressingly tender, and seasoned to perfection. It is also moistened with a mild eastern-style sauce that has just a little kick and a touch more sweetness than most barbecue sauces. The end result is absolutely delicious.

As word of Mitchell's barbecue spread, more customers showed up, making quarters at the restaurant increasingly cramped. Ed

Mitchell then started entertaining bigger dreams. He began building a much larger structure, a process that continued off and on for more than five years. Regular passers-by, who watched the walls rising ever so slowly, no doubt wondered if the project would ever be completed. In fact, hurricane winds blew the walls down twice.

Today, Mitchell is the proud owner of a virtual barbecue palace. There's a large, state-of-the-art kitchen, which contains wood-burning pits and an innovative and expensive ventilating system. There's a cafeteria-style dining room and another dining room with table service. There's a drive-through and a walk-up takeout window. There's a room with a square counter or bar with stools around the outside and a waist-high warming grate in the center— a "pig picking" bar, if you will. Finally, there's a wet bar and three rooms designed for private parties.

Ed Mitchell is fond of recalling a nightspot in the countryside near Wilson called "Tom's Place," where people went to visit, celebrate, and eat delicious food during his early years. Now, he's busy bringing that memory to life in his own establishment.

While the surroundings are much more spacious and modern than in the past, it's difficult to imagine that the food can possibly get any better than it always has been at Mitchell's. If you're out to experience a taste of rural Sunday dinners, covered-dish church suppers, down-home barbecues, and holiday celebrations of all kinds, this is a place that shouldn't be missed.

PARKER'S

2614 U.S. 301 South
Wilson, N.C. 27895
252-237-0972
Lunch and dinner daily

In earlier times, U.S. 301 was the equivalent of today's Interstate 95 for those traveling from the Northeast toward Florida. In 1946, Parker's was established alongside this main artery. At this location, it flourished in the transportation boom that followed World War II. For decades, it advertised itself as "North Carolina's Famous Eating Place."

Bobby Woodard and Don Williams, longtime former employees of the restaurant's founders, have owned the Parker's in Wilson since 1987. There is a restaurant with the same name in Greenville, which is operated as a totally separate business by some Parker family relatives.

A great majority of Parker's customers know in advance that they'll be ordering the restaurant's legendary mainstays: barbecue, fried chicken, Brunswick stew, corn sticks, and iced tea. The barbecue at the Wilson location comes from whole hogs, which are raised on the restaurant's own farm. The pork is cooked for hours on charcoal-burning pits. Gas burners mounted above the pits are lit during the last hour or so of cooking in order to brown and crisp the skin without having to turn the pigs.

The 'cue is solidly mainstream eastern-style fare: finely chopped; seasoned with salt, vinegar, and red pepper; and sprinkled liberally with crushed red pepper flakes. Because it comes from whole hogs rather than shoulders, it contains a higher percentage of white meat than Lexington-style barbecue. The extra white meat can make the chopped pork seem a bit dry, unless you add extra dashes of Parker's vinegar-based sauce, which is probably the standard against which all eastern sauces are measured.

Boiled potatoes and sweet yellow slaw are the unvarying accompaniments to the peppery barbecue. The golden-brown corn sticks make a delicious and functional implement for scooping up bites of Parker's sweet, traditional Brunswick stew. Often ordered in a combination dinner along with the barbecue and side dishes, Parker's fried chicken is as good as you'll find anywhere.

The restaurant has a 1960s feel about it, with scores of young men in white hats and white aprons waiting on tables. There are no waitresses. The décor is Spartan, but the food is considered by many to be fit for royalty.

BUNN'S BARBECUE
127 North King Street
Windsor, N.C. 27983
252-794-2274
Lunch and dinner (until 5:30 P.M.) Monday, Tuesday, Thursday, Friday
Lunch only (until 2:00 P.M.) Wednesday
Lunch and dinner (until 4:00 P.M.) Saturday

This intriguing little barbecue joint, located in a quaint mid-1800s building in historic downtown Windsor, has been selling barbecue since 1938, although not under its present name. It's a tiny place but one with self-confident owners, as evidenced by the fact that the place advertises its barbecue as "The World's Best."

Grace and Wilbur Russell bought the restaurant in 1969 and operate it with their sons, Russ and Randy. It seems that because the

Bunn's Barbecue in Windsor occupies a mid-1800s building that has been a doctor's office and a service station.

owner previous to the Russells was originally from the town of Bunn, in Franklin County, he was nicknamed "Bunn." Since everyone in Windsor was so accustomed to this name for the restaurant, the Russells decided to keep it.

Inside the one-time service station, there are a few tables where you can sit down at lunchtime, but the dinner trade (available only on days other than Wednesday) is mostly takeout. The barbecue, served with a spicy, vinegary sauce, is quintessential eastern-style, except that it's made from pork shoulders. Vinegar-based slaw and authentic Brunswick stew are popular, but instead of hush puppies, the really big deal here is the baked corn bread. Everyone wants a corner piece because of the crispy edges.

Barbecued chicken is available on Tuesday, and the Russells prepare chicken & pastry, an eastern North Carolina favorite, on Thursday. The restaurant is also well known for its hot dogs, which are available all the time, and for its homemade pies, including sweet-potato, chocolate, and coconut.

Remember, Bunn's closes at 2:00 P.M. on Wednesdays.

LITTLE RICHARD'S BARBECUE
4885 Country Club Road
Winston-Salem, N.C. 27104
336-760-3457
Lunch and dinner Monday through Saturday
Curb Service offered from 4:00 to 9:00 P.M.

Second location:
5389 Gumtree Road (Gumtree Road at N.C. 109)
Wallburg, N.C. 27373
336-769-4227
Lunch and dinner Monday through Saturday

Richard Berrier, who gained his barbecue experience in Lexington, started his first restaurant in Winston-Salem in 1991. He decided to open his establishment to keep people in Forsyth County from having to drive down to Davidson County to get real, Lexington-style barbecue.

There's some confusion surrounding the name "Little Richard's" in Winston-Salem, because aside from the original location on Country Club Road and a new restaurant in Wallburg, there's also a place called Little Richard's in Clemmons. There also used to be another on South Stratford Road before it changed its name. Without delving too far into complicated details of ownership and franchising-gone-awry, all you have to remember is that *great* barbecue, slow-cooked on real wood-burning pits, awaits you at

Little Richard's Barbecue wood-cooks on Winston-Salem's Country Club Road.

the restaurants on Country Club Road and Gumtree Road. The Clemmons restaurant is under different ownership.

By any measure, Richard's place on Country Club has to be regarded as one of the best barbecue restaurants in North Carolina. Rocking with music played at a higher-than-normal level, it's decorated with lots of old signs advertising cigarettes, soft drinks, and the like. The restaurant is laid-back, comfortable, and nearly always crowded. One of the most important decorations is a 1999 "certificate of barbecue excellence" from the North Carolina Barbecue Club.

The barbecue is pure Lexington style. It's pulled from pork shoulders, which are slow-roasted over wood coals for 12-14 hours. It has both a robust smoky flavor and the bewitching taste and aroma that come when juice drips onto coals spread directly beneath the meat. This process produces small clouds of aromatic steam that give the golden brown meat a grilled taste, which complements the overall smokiness. Whether it's coarse-chopped,

chopped, or sliced, the meat at Little Richard's is so tender that it practically falls apart without being chewed. The red barbecue slaw has just the right amount of zing to perfectly balance the sweet, pliant meat. On top of all that, the hush puppies are outstanding.

Little Richard's Lexington dip deflates the common misperception among easterners that Piedmont barbecue basically consists of "a hunk of dead hog meat with ketchup on it," as the Raleigh *News & Observer*'s Dennis Rogers once wrote. Typical of many Lexington dips, Richard's blend is still strongly vinegar-based, with a bracing dose of pepper. True, there's enough tomato to give it a soft-red color, but not nearly enough to turn it thick. There's just enough sugar to cut the power of the vinegar slightly. An additional hint of onion flavor will not lessen the taster's inevitable conclusion that the differences between eastern North Carolina sauce and Lexington dip are subtle indeed. As the label advises, the dip at Little Richard's reaches its peak flavor when it's heated, which is how it's served at the restaurant.

Little Richard's is also known for great burgers and a wide selection of other sandwiches. However, in my opinion, the barbecue is just too good here for anyone to wisely venture too far into other areas. As Little Richard's sauce label asserts, "Pig Connoisseurs Can't Be Wrong."

MR. BARBECUE

1381 Peters Creek Parkway
Winston-Salem, N.C. 27103
336-725-7827

Second location:
5954 University Parkway
Winston-Salem, N.C. 27105
336-377-3215

Both locations: Lunch and dinner Monday through Saturday

Since 1962, Mr. Barbecue on Peters Creek Parkway, which occupies a brick building with brightly painted red-and-white accents, has been cooking barbecue over real wood coals. A second location on University Parkway resembles a fast-food joint at first glance, but behind the boxy, vinyl-sided structure, the reassuring sight of a big brick chimney and a pile of split wood indicates that a real, old-fashioned interaction between pig and fire is going on here—at least some of the time. The Peters Creek location (and, I suspect, the University Parkway restaurant, as well,) has added a couple of electric pits to augment the wood-burning ones, so the degree of genuine pit-cooked taste you experience at either place probably depends on the day and the hour you're there. The paper wrappers for the barbecue sandwiches don't make a distinction about how they're prepared, since they're all imprinted with the words "real hickory wood barbecue."

Personally, I don't quite understand why a restaurateur wouldn't either make a decision to stick with the wood-burning pits all the way or convert entirely to the electric version. Some places use electric pits only as backup when they get extremely busy, but that means that even on the same day, some of the customers are going to get a very different-tasting product than others. The same customer is also likely to have two entirely different experiences on different occasions, and if there's one thing that barbecue customers value, it's knowing what to expect and what they can truthfully recommend to others. If cooking with wood is worth the trouble at all, it's worth doing all the time. On the other hand, an owner who thinks the public really can't tell the difference might just as well go with electricity and be done with it.

I sampled a coarse-chopped sandwich at both locations and enjoyed them both. On University Parkway, I found the bun soft, the meat tender, and the dip mild and appealing. There was a delightful peppery aftertaste, but there didn't seem to be a great deal of smoke flavor, especially considering the fact that I had just seen a woodpile behind the restaurant. On Peters Creek (on this particular Saturday, anyway), hickory smoke was wafting across the parking lot, and I actually observed one of the cooks putting wood into the pit's firebox. As I anticipated, the meat was *very* smoky tasting and delicious. Everything else about the sandwich matched the one I'd had earlier at the University location, which illustrates my point about the advisability of customers knowing what they're going to get at any particular time.

Both places have tasty ribs and a choice of fried or barbecued chicken. Both are also known for their terrific hot dogs. The peach cobbler at the Peters Creek restaurant had a lazy man's "dump cake" crust, made basically by sprinkling a dry cake mix on top of the fruit filling, but it was still worthwhile. I noticed several people ordering the homemade banana pudding with meringue topping at the University location.

At its best, Mr. Barbecue offers delicious, tender, *smoky* barbecue, and at other times it serves moist, tender barbecue with little pit-cooked flavor. Maybe it would make an impression on the owner if we all started asking right up front whether the barbecue we're getting at that moment is from the wood-burning pits or the electric ovens.

PIG PICKIN'S OF AMERICA

613 Deacon Boulevard
Winston-Salem, N.C. 27106
336-777-0105
Lunch and dinner Monday through Saturday

Two other locations:

3650 Reynolda Road
Winston-Salem, N.C. 27106
336-923-2285
(Limited menu, but open for lunch on Sunday)

548 South Stratford Rd.
Winston-Salem, N.C. 27103
336-722-7675
Lunch and dinner Monday through Saturday

Pig Pickin's has been at the same location on Deacon Boulevard, near Lawrence Joel Coliseum, since 1985. Over the years, the restaurant's concept has evolved so that it now includes a distinctly western décor; both pork and beef barbecue, chicken, and ribs; Mexican entreés; a large selection of wines and beers; and even mixed drinks. In days past, the only liquor available at North Carolina barbecue joints was consumed out of jugs and mason jars in the parking lot.

Despite what you might think about the western and Mexican

influences, the people at Pig Pickin's have always operated with a solid understanding of Tar Heel barbecue. That may be due to the fact that it was begun by someone with real experience—the son of the owner of Mr. Barbecue, which is located on Peters Creek Parkway in Winston-Salem. However, North Carolina's barbecue heritage isn't very well reflected in the choice of decorative items, which range from Indian blankets to a stuffed coyote. The addition of so many different kinds of foods not normally considered barbecue in these parts, such as beef brisket, ribs, and chicken and pork barbecue burritos, might lead to the impression that the proprietors consider one type of barbecue just about as good as another. *Heresy!*

Despite any misgivings created, the pork barbecue at Pig Pickin's is really pretty good. The menu advertises "hickory *smoked* barbecue," but there's no sign of a real pit or a woodpile. This leads to the conclusion that the barbecue is probably cooked in electric smokers, rather than on open pits. As I've mentioned elsewhere, what's missing in this process is the extra flavor that comes when juice drips directly onto coals beneath the pork. However, it is possible to achieve brown crusting, distinctive flavor, and a nice reddish tinge to the meat in this type smoker. I admit that I enjoyed the taste of the pork at Pig Pickin's without any real reservations. The sauce here really is a tomato-based concoction without much of a vinegar tang. I personally thought it was a little too sweet. However, the tender, flavorful pork, the barbecue slaw, and the sauce all go nicely with a soft, white bun, producing a barbecue sandwich that would be quite acceptable anywhere.

I understand from others I've talked to that the beef brisket is worth trying. The word is that the cooks simmer the brisket in stock for a few hours before finishing it in the smoker.

Pig Pickin's also has quite a few salad choices, specialty sandwiches with a western accent, and a pretty extensive dessert selection.

You'll actually enjoy the slightly skewed take on North Carolina barbecue culture you'll find at Pig Pickin's, but I have to say you'll also enjoy the food just fine.

WILD HOGS BARBECUE
5910 University Parkway
Winston-Salem, N.C. 27105
336-377-3550
Lunch and dinner Monday through Saturday

The name of this place used to be "Hogs Wild," but a change in ownership brought a change in name. Now the visual symbol of the place is a group of pigs dressed in biker gear, riding large motorcycles, which are also called "hogs." Let me hasten to add that bikers do not frequent the place, so no one should feel intimidated about coming in and enjoying some really good barbecue.

While checking out the pit in back, I noticed that the woodpile was quite depleted, indicating that someone had been doing a lot of cooking recently. That is always a really good sign. I was further heartened to see this note on the menu: "All food is prepared fresh as ordered. Expect wings, steaks and burgers to take a little longer. Due to cooking on a pit the old fashioned way, some redness may appear in the barbecue or chicken." V-r-o-o-o-m, v-r-o-o-o-m, my motor was already at full throttle!

The very tender, flavorful coarse-chopped barbecue is served with hush puppies and a choice of red or white slaw. I also sampled the pit-cooked ribs, which are available only on Thursday, Friday, and Saturday. The ribs, which are falling-off-the-bone tender, are glazed with a thick, molasses-flavored sauce. While thick sauces of this type may not be considered appropriate for chopped barbecue in North Carolina, there are no real rules or traditions regarding rib sauces, and my own personal preference is the thicker the sauce, the better. Wild Hogs also has its own version of the popular deep-fried whole onion appetizer. Here it's called a "hog's head."

Basically Wild Hogs advertises Lexington-style barbecue, ribs, and chicken. The chicken is pit cooked on Friday and Saturday only. The menu also indicates a selection of burgers, steaks, hamburger steaks, hot dogs, and sandwiches. In addition, there are some appealing daily specials—chicken pie on Monday; country-style steak on Tuesday; pork tenderloin and gravy on Wednesday; salmon cakes on Thursday; and meat loaf on Friday.

Be advised that the restaurant is a little hard to find. It sits back from the street, more or less hidden behind a Japanese restaurant, a Mexican eatery, and a fried-chicken place. It's located beside the King's Inn motel, just west of the intersection of University Parkway and U.S. 52 North.

TWO BROTHERS BAR-B-Q RESTAURANT
2711 Mill Street
Winterville, N.C. 28590
252-353-4200
Lunch and dinner Monday through Saturday

Two Brothers is a surprise find in the little town of Winterville, which is practically a suburb of Greenville.

One surprise is that the place is there at all. Since it's in the

Winterville "business district," off heavily traveled N.C. 11, it's practically invisible to many people. Even in my extensive search for barbecue establishments, I hadn't heard of it in my travels around the Greenville area until recently.

The other surprise is that in the heart of eastern North Carolina, which is vinegar-and-pepper country, the place advertises "Lexington-style red sauce." Since there are at least a couple of places in the western half of the state that advertise eastern barbecue for the benefit of transplants from the coastal plain, it probably shouldn't be surprising that someone had the idea of doing Lexington-style barbecue for westerners who've moved east.

One very welcome sign is that Two Brothers cooks its barbecue over real, live charcoal in a pit house that's separated from the main building. Maybe the influence of Bum's Barbecue and the Skylight Inn in nearby Ayden, both of which pit-cook over real wood, extends up the road a few miles to Winterville. At any rate, the presence of these three restaurants helps counterbalance the prevailing trend in eastern Carolina toward electric and gas-fired barbecue pits. As for those who say charcoal falls short of real wood, I'm personally convinced from my own hands-on experience that this is largely a myth. If handled and lit correctly, charcoal can provide all the smoke flavor anyone could desire, especially if a few wood chunks are used in addition.

The barbecue I ordered was well seasoned and tender. It had enough pit-cooked flavor to set it apart from the generic barbecue that's so prevalent in the east. I didn't think the sauce could really be classified as a Lexington-style dip, since it wasn't all that different from several other eastern sauces I've tasted. The mere fact that the menu called it "sauce" rather than "dip," which is the common term used around Lexington, should have served as a clue. In any case, the sauce is perfectly good and complements the meat nicely.

I also tried the house barbecued chicken, which had a good smoky taste and color, although I didn't think the Kraft-style "chicken" sauce added much. What did add a great deal to my enjoyment of the meal was a serving of wonderful collard greens, along with some authentic, eastern-style boiled potatoes. You can also choose from a variety of other vegetables as well.

Two Brothers is a clean, attractive place, where you can order ribs, fried chicken, and other specialties in addition to the barbecue.

Just follow the signs from N.C. 11 to the tiny Winterville downtown area to experience some barbecue that reflects extra time and effort.

HOLDEN'S BARBECUE
528 U.S. 1
Youngsville, N.C. 27596
919-556-3607
Lunch (until 2:00 P.M.) Monday through Thursday and also on Saturday
Lunch and dinner on Friday

This unprepossessing little place is located in a two-room, yellow cinder-block building on U.S. 1, north of Wake Forest and a short distance across the Franklin County line. The restaurant's name is printed on a weathered plastic sign originally designed to promote Pine State Ice Cream. While Pine State is now out of business, Holden's is still going strong, as it has been since 1964.

The main attraction here is genuine eastern-style, wood-cooked barbecue. Even though the restaurant uses shoulders, rather than the whole hog, the meat is seasoned on a par with the east's best barbecue. To begin with, it's properly salted; the meat has tiny bits of fat chopped into it, which serve as the real conduit for the smoky, pit-cooked flavor; and it contains just the right amount of ground red pepper and red-pepper flakes. A well-balanced, vinegar-based sauce adds the perfect finishing touch. White coleslaw, moistened with vinegar and sugar (no mayonnaise), and coarse and crispy hush puppies round out the meal. Sliced pig-picking-style pork barbecue is also available, as is barbecued chicken that's already been pulled off the bone.

I found the restaurant's Brunswick stew to be pleasant tasting, if a little watery. Despite the fact that it contained both garden peas and carrots (*soup* ingredients!), the overall effect was positive.

When you're not in a barbecue frame of mind, you can find other choices at Holden's, including fried chicken, seafood, hamburger steaks, chicken and dumplings, and various sandwiches. There's banana pudding on Wednesday and Friday; and homemade sweet-potato, chocolate, and coconut pie (for as long as it lasts) on the other days.

Stopping at Holden's will leave you with the fulfilling realization that you've had a sure-'nough, eastern "bobbycue" experience.

Smithfield Chicken 'N' Bar-B-Q

10414 U.S. 70 West
Clayton, N.C. 27520
919-553-4553

Harnett Crossing Shopping Center (Exit 73 off Interstate 95)
Dunn, N.C. 28334
910-892-2693

5539 Camden Road
Fayetteville, N.C. 28306
910-426-9515

9515 Cliffdale Road
Fayetteville, N.C. 28304
910-826-9622

5180 N.C. 42 West (Exit 312 off Interstate 40)
Garner, N.C. 27529
919-773-0774

4000 Jones Sausage Road (Exit 303 off Interstate 40)
Garner, N.C. 27529
919-779-0095

1419 East Main Street (U.S. 70 East)
Havelock, N.C. 28532
252-447-5885

1105 Gum Branch Road
Jacksonville, N.C. 28540
910-347-6355

315 Western Boulevard
Jacksonville, N.C. 28546
910-353-9595

402 Plaza Road
Laurinburg, N.C. 28352
910-266-8700

5050 Fayetteville Road
Lumberton, N.C. 28358
910-618-9542

4114 Arendell Street (U.S. 70)
Morehead City, N.C. 28557
252-247-7476

2607 Dr. Martin Luther King, Jr. Boulevard (U.S.70 & U.S. 17)
New Bern, N.C. 28562
252-636-2398

1380 Harnett Dunn Highway (Exit 341 off Interstate 40)
Newton Grove, N.C. 28366
910-594-0415

7911 Fayetteville Road
Raleigh, N.C. 27603
919-661-9151

924 Brightleaf Boulevard
Smithfield, N.C. 27577
919-934-8721

2669 N.C. 42 West
Warsaw, N.C. 28398
910-293-2218

7300 Market Street
Wilmington, N.C. 28411
910-686-4175

Triangle East Shopping Center
Zebulon, N.C. 27597
919-269-7009

All locations: Lunch and dinner daily

I have to admit that I avoided Smithfield's for a long time because it was a chain and because I was more interested in family-run places that had interesting stories surrounding them.

The fact is, though, that these folks serve eastern-style barbecue that's every bit as good as that found in some of the most famous barbecue houses of the coastal plain, perhaps better than some. Here you'll find barbecue that's prepared without a hint of any wood smoke, but it's tender, perfectly seasoned, and, most importantly, not chopped too finely. The meat has an attractive, chunky texture that allows it to retain its natural moisture. As a result, it is much more pleasant *al dente* (to the tooth).

The vinegar sauce is right on target, considering that this is very much an eastern North Carolina chain, and the portions are more than generous.

I enjoyed the sweet yellow slaw that accompanies the barbecue. While the other side dish, the potato salad, had perhaps a bit too much mayonnaise for my personal taste, it still comes across as tangy and appealing. Hush puppies at Smithfield's are fresh, hot, and not too sweet.

I'm happy to report that the fried chicken matches the pork barbecue in quality. It has a crispy coating and skin, a moist and juicy interior, and perfect seasonings. At the time I visited, these restaurants were also offering whole, deep-fried turkey breasts. Although I did not sample this dish, it should be excellent as well, considering the superior taste of the chicken.

I found the iced tea to be superb. In fact, it was better than that served at many of the "name" barbecue joints. However, the pre-packaged desserts are merely a concession to convenience and are not worth your time.

The restaurant sells both its chicken breader and its barbecue sauce at each location.

For the consistently high quality of the food, generous portions, reasonable prices, and cleanliness, Smithfield's gets a good, strong

"B-plus" or even an "A-minus" in my grade book, and I look forward to going back.

INDEX